Writing Empirical Research Reports: A Basic Guide for Students of the Social and Behavioral Sciences, Ninth Edition, offers clear and practical guidance on how to write research proposals, reports, theses, and dissertations.

The book describes the types of information that should be included, how this information should be expressed, and where various types of information should be placed within a research report. The organization is designed to walk students through all the elements required when writing an original research report for a class, for a thesis/dissertation, or for publication. Most guidelines are illustrated with examples from actual (and recent) research reports published in peer-reviewed journals across the social and behavioral sciences. The new edition includes fully updated examples and chapter exercises, expanded material on qualitative methods, significant new material on research ethics, and new content on online research including social media.

Accompanied by online resources for students and instructors, *Writing Empirical Research Reports* is ideal for use in research methods courses, thesis/dissertation preparation courses, research seminars where writing a research report is a culminating activity, and any graduate-level seminar in which the instructor covers the vital components necessary to prepare a research manuscript for submission for publication.

Melisa C. Galvan (Ph.D., 2013, UC Berkeley) is co-author of *Writing Literature Reviews: A Guide for Students of the Social and Behavioral Sciences* (Routledge, 2017) and *Proposing Empirical Research: A Guide to the Fundamentals* (Routledge, 2020). Dr. Galvan is Associate Professor at California State University, Northridge.

Writing Empirical Research Reports

A Basic Guide for Students of the Social and Behavioral Sciences

Ninth Edition

Melisa C. Galvan and Fred Pyrczak

Routledge
Taylor & Francis Group

NEW YORK AND LONDON

Designed cover image: jakkaje808 / Getty Images

Ninth edition published 2024
by Routledge
605 Third Avenue, New York, NY 10158

and by Routledge
4 Park Square, Milton Park, Abingdon, Oxon, OX14 4RN

Routledge is an imprint of the Taylor & Francis Group, an informa business

© 2024 Taylor & Francis

First edition published by Pyrczak Publishing 1992
Eighth edition published by Routledge 2017

ISBN: 978-1-032-13678-3 (hbk)
ISBN: 978-1-032-13680-6 (pbk)
ISBN: 978-1-003-23041-0 (ebk)

DOI: 10.4324/9781003230410

Typeset in Bembo
by SPi Technologies India Pvt Ltd (Straive)

Access the Support Material: www.routledge.com/9781032136806

To Bernie and Emma Cristina – my eternal love and appreciation for you both goes beyond words.

Contents

Contents

Contents

Contents

Contents

Contents

Introduction to the Ninth Edition

This text presents guidelines frequently followed by writers of empirical research reports. The guidelines describe the types of information that should typically be included, how this information should be expressed, and where various types of information should be placed within a research report.

The intended audience of this book are students whose research reports are expected to mirror the writing of a peer-reviewed journal. Depending on a writer's field, "empirical research report" could take on different meanings and reports may need to be written to reflect a different audience. While scholars and students in the social sciences do empirical research, their reports may be prepared for different types of audiences including, but not limited to, private clients or nongovernmental organizations (NGOs).

Irregardless, the overall goal of a research report is to provide a coherent and credible response to a specific research problem. As will be discussed, each section of the report is intended to help the author(s) meet that goal.

Students whose professors require them to write research-based term papers that resemble journal articles will find this text especially useful. The exercises at the end of each chapter are designed to provide practice for their use. Graduate students who are in the process of writing theses and dissertations will find that the guidelines also apply to their writing and pointers for such students are interspersed throughout the text.

New to This Edition

When *Writing Empirical Research Reports* was first published in 1992 the process of undertaking an empirical research report was very different. Students and researchers relied on brick-and-mortar university libraries, including their paper cataloguing systems, as the primary means with which to access published scholarly research. Today, researchers from around the world can choose to conduct their literature searches and data collection entirely online, utilizing the many online search databases and online repositories of information available to scholars.

DOI: 10.4324/9781003230410-1   1

The book has been updated to reflect this turn with the addition of a new co-author with extensive expertise teaching and mentoring students in the digital age.

Assumptions Underlying This Text

It is assumed that students have access (either in print form or online) to a traditional style manual such as the *Publication Manual of the American Psychological Association* (APA), which prescribes mechanical details for research writing. It is also assumed that students have already identified a research topic, applied sound research methods, and analyzed their data. These topics are not covered in this book.

Considerations in Using This Text

The guidelines presented in this text are based on generalizations that the authors reached while reading extensively in journals in the social and behavioral sciences. If you are a student using this text for a research class or independent study, your professor may ask you to modify some of the guidelines. This may occur for two reasons. First, as a learning experience, a professor may require students to do certain things that go beyond the preparation of a paper for possible publication. For instance, we suggest that the literature review for a journal article be highly selective. However, a professor may require their students to write a comprehensive literature review to demonstrate that they have conducted a broad search of the literature on a given topic. Second, as in all types of writing, there is a certain amount of subjectivity concerning what constitutes effective writing; even experts may have differing opinions. Fortunately, these differences are less pronounced in scientific writing than in many other types of writing.

Experienced writers may violate many of the guidelines presented in this text and still write publishable and effective research reports. Beginners are encouraged to follow the guidelines closely until they have mastered the art of scientific writing.

Where to Begin in This Text

For a quick overview of five fundamental principles for effective research writing, it is recommended that you begin with Appendix B, "Thinking Straight and Writing That Way." Then read Chapter 1, which will provide an overview of the structure of typical empirical research reports.

Organization

The organization of this book is designed to walk students through all the elements required when writing an empirical research report.

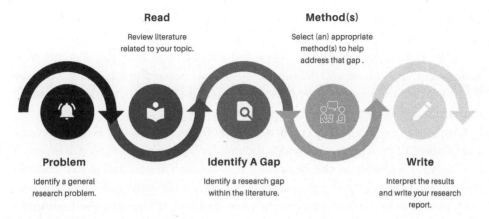

Figure 1 The Research Process.

The research process (see Figure 1) and writing process are very different. As such, the writing of a research report may occur in a different order than is outlined in this book, and that is okay. However, the chapters of this text are organized to mirror the order by which a student may choose to undertake the writing of their research report. This is purposely different than the order of the core components of an empirical research report (see Figure 2).

Chapter 1 begins with a general overview of the structure of typical empirical research reports. Chapters 2, 3, and 4 discuss the process of identifying, writing, and refining hypotheses and research questions. This is intended to provide students with a strong foundation to begin their writing.

The rest of the book follows the general structure of an empirical research report. Chapter 5 addresses the key elements necessary to consider when writing a title.

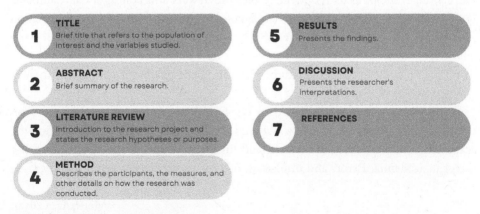

Figure 2 Components of a Research Report.

Chapter 6 outlines the purpose of an introduction and literature review in a research report. Chapter 7 presents guidelines on what to define and how to write definitions.

Authors of research published in journal articles often integrate statements of assumptions, limitations, and delimitations—a topic covered in Chapter 8. Chapter 9 outlines the components of a Method section and Chapter 10 explores the topic of describing different types of experimental methods.

Chapter 11 outlines the key components of both the Analysis and Results sections and Chapter 12 presents guidelines for writing the last section of a research report.

Chapter 13 returns to the beginning of a research report and walks students through the process of writing an abstract. Chapter 14 is dedicated to key components present in research reports specific to qualitative and mixed methods research. Chapter 15 presents general guidelines for preparing a reference list.

Appendix A is intended to serve as a checklist that students can follow and double-check when writing their own reports. Appendix B presents the first-hand perspective of an academic and journal editor who has reviewed and critiqued many research manuscripts. Finally, Appendix C serves as a brief reference guide on significance testing and the null hypothesis.

About the Examples in This Text

Most of the guidelines are illustrated with examples from research reports published in academic journals. References for these examples are indicated with endnotes. Complete bibliographic references can be found in the References section near the end of this book. Examples without endnotes were written by the authors to illustrate selected guidelines.

Acknowledgments

Dr. Galvan is thankful to Routledge's blind reviewers and colleagues at California State University, Northridge for their helpful comments throughout the revision process. She is also grateful to the CSUN College of Humanities for funding the sabbatical and release time needed to see this new edition to completion. A special thank you is due to Routledge editor Hannah Shakespeare, for her trust, patience, and good counsel over the years.

Dr. Galvan is especially indebted to Dr. Fred Pyrczak for his original work on this book. She spent her summers as a high school and college student learning the academic publishing trade from him, and his mentorship has indelibly shaped her career in academia. Errors and omissions, of course, remain her responsibility.

Melisa C. Galvan
Associate Professor
California State University, Northridge

Chapter 1

Structuring a Research Report

This chapter provides a general overview of the elements typically included in research reports. Each of these is discussed in greater detail in subsequent chapters.

➢ Guideline 1.1 A research report typically has a brief title

Titles of published research reports are typically brief. They usually refer to the population/sample of interest and to the variables studied. Example 1.1.1 shows a title of about average length for a research report published in an academic journal. In it, the variables are self-esteem and employment status. The population consists of individuals with autism.

Example 1.1.1

The Relationship between Self-Esteem and Employment Status among Individuals with Autism

---

Writing titles is discussed in more detail in Chapter 5.

➢ Guideline 1.2 An abstract usually follows the title

An abstract is a brief summary of the research contained within the report. It is often stated in 150 to 250 words. A typical abstract summarizes the purpose of the study, the methods used to conduct the research, and the results.

An abstract is typically written after a complete draft of the report has been completed. Hence, guidelines for writing abstracts are presented near the end of this book in Chapter 13.

DOI: 10.4324/9781003230410-2   5

➤ **Guideline 1.3 The body of a typical research report begins with a literature review, which serves as the introduction to the research project**

In research reports published in academic journals, the literature review is presented just below the abstract. Literature is cited in order to (1) establish the importance of the research problem, (2) inform the readers about what is known and what is not known about the problem, and (3) establish the need for the research described in the rest of the research report. The literature review concludes with a statement of the specific research hypotheses or purposes.

In theses and dissertations, the literature review serves the same purpose as the literature review in reports of research in journals. However, it is traditional to begin a thesis or dissertation with an introduction in the first chapter, which presents the researcher's rationale for conducting the study and has relatively few citations to literature. This is followed by a second chapter that presents an extensive literature review.

Writing introductions and literature reviews is covered in Chapter 6. Writing research hypotheses and objectives is covered in Chapters 2–4.

➤ **Guideline 1.4 The Method section describes the participants, the measures, and other details on how the research was conducted**

The Method section immediately follows the literature review. At a minimum, it has two subheadings: "Participants" (sometimes called "Sample") and "Measures" (sometimes called "Instrumentation").

The subsection on the participants describes how they were identified and selected. The subsection on measures describes the instruments (e.g., tests, online surveys, attitude scales, interview schedules) that were used to collect the data.

A third (optional) subheading, "Procedure," is sometimes included. This is the appropriate place to describe the treatments given in an experiment or any other steps taken to execute the research that were not already described under "Participants" or "Measures."

A fourth (optional) subheading, "Analysis," is sometimes included. This is used to discuss the selection of methods of analysis.[1]

Guidelines for writing Method sections are described in Chapters 9 and 10 and the first part of Chapter 11.

Example 1.4.1 shows the structure of a basic research report with the elements discussed up to this point in this chapter.

Example 1.4.1

Title in Upper- and Lowercase Letters
Abstract (a main heading; centered in bold)[2]
A literature review that introduces the research problem (with no heading)
Method (a main heading; centered in bold)
Participants (a subheading; flush left in bold**)**
Measures (a subheading; flush left in bold)
Procedure (optional; a subheading; flush left in bold)
Analysis (optional; a subheading; flush left in bold)

➤ Guideline 1.5 The Results section presents the findings

The Results section immediately follows the Method section. It has a major heading of "Results" and is centered. (See Example 1.7.1.)

In reports on quantitative research, the Results section is usually brief. Often, statistics are presented in tables or figures with a discussion of how they shed light on the research hypotheses or purposes.

In reports on qualitative research, the Results section can be quite lengthy. In this section, qualitative researchers describe the major themes revealed by the participants' responses. These are usually illustrated with direct quotations from the participants.

Chapter 11 describes how to write Results sections, and Chapter 14 examines writing results for qualitative research in more detail.

➤ Guideline 1.6 The Discussion section presents the researcher's interpretations

The Discussion section immediately follows the Results section. It has a major heading of "Discussion" and is centered.[3] (See Example 1.7.1.) In long research reports, the Discussion section might begin with a brief summary of the methods and results of the research. In addition, researchers use this section to reflect on the results and their relationship to the research hypotheses and purposes. This section also often includes (1) a statement of the limitations of the research (e.g., weaknesses in the research methodology), (2) implications of the findings, and (3) suggested directions for future research.

Guidelines for writing the Discussion section are described in Chapter 12.

➤ Guideline 1.7 The reference list should contain references only to literature cited in the report

References for all the research cited within a report are listed under the main heading "References" (centered in bold). The reference list should not be a suggested reading list. It should only contain references to literature directly cited within the research report. A "Bibliography" may be used instead of a "References" list if you wish to provide all the sources consulted to generate your ideas about the topic. Like a "References" list, a "Bibliography" must also include all references cited within your report. APA publications generally require reference lists, not bibliographies. The preparation of a reference list is described in Chapter 15.

Example 1.7.1 shows the structure of a basic research report (without the optional subheadings discussed under Guideline 1.4).

Example 1.7.1

Title in Upper- and Lowercase Letters

Abstract (a main heading; centered in bold)

A literature review that introduces the research problem (with no heading)

Method (a main heading; centered in bold)

Participants (a subheading; flush left in bold)

Measures (a subheading; flush left in bold)

Results (a main heading; centered in bold)

Discussion (a main heading; centered in bold)

References (a main heading; centered in bold)

Note that the technical name for a main heading is *first-level heading*, while the technical name for a subheading under a main heading is *second-level heading*. Headings under a second-level heading are called *third-level headings*, which are discussed under the next guideline.

➤ Guideline 1.8 In long reports, use additional second- and third-level headings

In long research reports (or long sections within reports), consider using additional headings to help guide readers. For instance, in a long Discussion section, these second-level headings might be used: "Summary," "Limitations," "Implications," and "Directions for Future Research."

Third-level headings might be used under second-level ones. For instance, under the second-level heading of "Measures," these third-level headings might be used:

"Construction of the Measures," "Validity of the Measures," and "Administration of the Measures."

The three levels of headings for the Method section of a research report are illustrated in Example 1.8.1. Note that third-level headings end with a period.

Example 1.8.1

        Method (a *first-level* heading; centered in bold)
Participants (a *second-level* heading; flush left in bold)
Measures (a *second-level* heading; flush left in bold)
    Construction of the Measures. (a *third-level* heading; indented in bold, ends with a period)
    Validity of the Measures. (a *third-level* heading; indented in bold, ends with a period)
    Administration of the Measures. (a *third-level* heading; indented in bold, ends with a period)

As a general rule, longer sections of research reports should have more second- and third-level headings than shorter sections.

Concluding Comments

The essential elements in a research report are the title, abstract, introduction, literature review, a description of research methods, a section that presents results, and a discussion. Additional headings and subheadings may be used as needed for clarity.

Note that researchers also present ethical protocols, definitions, as well as descriptions of their assumptions in their research reports. These may be integrated within various sections of a report. Guidelines for writing these elements are presented in Chapters 7–8.

Exercises for Chapter 1

Part A

1. Titles of research reports usually refer to what two elements?

2. What is an "abstract"?

3. How many words does an "abstract" usually contain?

4. According to this chapter, literature is cited in order to establish the importance of the research problem and to inform readers about what is known and what is not known about the problem. What other purposes do citations serve?

5. At a minimum, the Method section has what two subheadings (second-level headings)?

6. What does a Measures section describe?

7. The Results section immediately follows what other section?

8. Suggested directions for future research are presented in which section?

Part B

Identify two reports of research recently published in online academic journals and answer the following questions:

9. Were the titles and abstracts "brief" or "lengthy"? Explain.

10. Were the headings and subheadings consistent with what you expected to find based on your reading of this chapter? Explain.

Part C

For those working on a thesis or dissertation, please identify an example of a completed thesis or dissertation. Then, answer the following questions:

11. Are the introduction and literature review presented in separate chapters?

12. List all the chapter titles. Do they correspond to the headings described in this chapter?

Notes

1 This subheading is most common in reports on qualitative research (see Chapter 14) because methods for qualitative analysis are not standardized. In quantitative research reports, the selection of a standard method of statistical analysis usually does not need to be discussed.

2 This heading is commonly found and used in unpublished papers. In research journals, it is often omitted, with the abstract being identified by its placement at the beginning and by being indented on the left and right.

3 While this section can have various names, such as "Discussion and Conclusions," "Summary and Discussion," and "Discussion and Implications," the one-word heading "Discussion" is the most common.

Chapter 2

Writing Simple Research Hypotheses

Often, the purpose of a research project is to test a research hypothesis (e.g., gather data that shed light on the validity of a hypothesis).

In a single sentence, a simple research hypothesis describes the results that a researcher expects to find. In effect, it is a prediction. The following are guidelines for writing this type of hypothesis.

➤ **Guideline 2.1 A simple research hypothesis should name two variables and indicate the type of relationship expected between them**

In Example 2.1.1, the variables are "psychomotor coordination" and "self-esteem." The researcher expects to find higher self-esteem among individuals with better psychomotor coordination as well as lower self-esteem among those with less coordination.

Example 2.1.1

There is a predicted relationship between level of psychomotor coordination and degree of self-esteem.

In Example 2.1.2, "length of light deprivation" is a stimulus or independent variable, which will be manipulated by the researcher. The hypothesis suggests that some rats will be deprived of light for longer than others. The second variable is "performance in a maze task," which is an outcome or dependent variable. The hypothesis indicates that the researcher expects to find longer periods of light deprivation associated with poorer maze performance.

Example 2.1.2

Among rats, length of light deprivation from birth is inversely associated with performance in a maze task.

Example 2.1.3 also contains an independent variable: the type of homework assignment (online versus paper submission). The anticipated relationship of this variable to students' enthusiasm for doing homework is clear in the hypothesis. Note that the students' enthusiasm for doing homework is the dependent variable (e.g., outcome).

Example 2.1.3

Students who are administered self-correcting homework assignments online have more enthusiasm for doing homework than students who are given paper submission homework assignments.

In Example 2.1.4, two variables are named, but the expected relationship between them is not stated. The improved version of Example 2.1.4 makes it clear that the researcher believes that those with more free-floating anxiety have less ability to form friendships.

Example 2.1.4

College students differ in their levels of free-floating anxiety, and they differ in their ability to form friendships.

Improved Version of Example 2.1.4

Among college students, there is an inverse relationship between level of free-floating anxiety and ability to form friendships.

➤ **Guideline 2.2 When there is an independent variable,
name a specific dependent variable**

As indicated in the previous guideline, some studies have independent variables, which are sets of treatments that are manipulated by researchers. The outcome that results from a set of treatments is known as the dependent variable. The purpose of such a study (known as an experiment) is to determine the effects of the independent variable on the dependent variable.

The hypothesis for an experiment should name a specific dependent variable. In Example 2.2.1, the independent variable is the use of guest speakers. Furthermore, the phrase "more effective" implies that there is a dependent variable, which is not specified. The improved version specifies that the dependent variable is the number of career choices that the participants are willing to consider.

Example 2.2.1

Career counseling supplemented with guest speakers holding various occupations is more effective than career counseling without guest speakers.

Improved Version of Example 2.2.1

Participants receiving career counseling supplemented with guest speakers holding various occupations are willing to consider a larger number of career choices than participants who receive career counseling without guest speakers.

Because the purpose of all experiments is to determine the effects of the independent variable on a dependent variable, you need to be specific about how the effects will be analyzed. It is never enough to say that the dependent variable will have an *effect* or be *more effective*. In other words, the specific behavior that will be used to judge effectiveness (e.g., number of career choices considered) should be explicitly mentioned.

Example 2.2.2 also fails to name a specific dependent variable (e.g., "better off" is not specific enough). The improved version specifies that "lower blood pressure readings" is the dependent variable.

Example 2.2.2

Middle-aged males who regularly exercise vigorously are better off than those who do not exercise vigorously.

Improved Version of Example 2.2.2

Middle-aged males who regularly exercise vigorously have lower blood pressure readings than those who do not exercise vigorously.

➤ Guideline 2.3 Consider naming population(s) in the hypothesis

This guideline is especially applicable when (1) a relationship is expected only in a particular population, (2) the study deals with a population that previously has been unstudied, and (3) the focus of the study is on the comparison of two or more populations.

In Example 2.3.1, "children aged 5 to 7" are identified as the researcher's population of interest.

Example 2.3.1

Among children aged 5 to 7, there is a direct relationship between level of psychomotor coordination and degree of self-esteem.

In Example 2.3.2, "student nurses" are identified as the researcher's population of interest.

Example 2.3.2

Student nurses who receive app-based training in calculating drug dosages make fewer calculation errors than student nurses who do not receive app-based training.

In Example 2.3.3, two populations of high school students that will be compared (e.g., those with private transportation and those who use public transportation) are named in the hypothesis.

Example 2.3.3

High school students who have private transportation participate in more extracurricular activities than high school students who must take public transportation.

➤ Guideline 2.4 A simple hypothesis should usually be expressed in a single sentence

The hypothesis in Example 2.4.1 violates this guideline because it is stated in two sentences. This is corrected in the improved version.

Example 2.4.1

Social anxiety may impede the performance of college students in public speaking classes. As a result, students with such anxiety will perform more poorly in such classes.

Improved Version of Example 2.4.1

Students with high levels of social anxiety exhibit poorer speech-giving performance than students with low levels of social anxiety.

> ### Guideline 2.5 Even a simple hypothesis should be as specific as possible within a single sentence

The improved version of Example 2.5.1 is more specific than the original because the meaning of "cell phone use" (e.g., use of FaceTime) and the meaning of "well-being" (e.g., reported levels of loneliness) are indicated in the improved version.

Example 2.5.1

There is an inverse relationship between cell phone use and well-being among the elderly.

Improved Version of Example 2.5.1

There is an inverse relationship between elderly individuals' use of FaceTime and their reported levels of loneliness.

Likewise, the improved version of Example 2.5.2 is more specific than the original version because the improved version indicates that being "better administrators" will be measured in terms of employees' perceptions of leadership qualities. Also, the improved version is more specific because it indicates that two types of administrators will be compared.

Example 2.5.2

Administrators who provide wellness programs for their employees are perceived as better administrators.

> ***Improved Version of Example 2.5.2***
>
> Administrators who provide wellness programs for their employees receive higher employee ratings on selected leadership qualities than administrators who do not provide such programs.

Deciding how specific to make a hypothesis is a subjective matter because it is usually not possible to provide full definitions of all terms in the single sentence that states a hypothesis. Instead, complete definitions should be provided elsewhere in a research report. Guidelines for writing definitions are presented in Chapter 7.

➤ Guideline 2.6 If a comparison is to be made, the elements to be compared should be stated

Comparisons start with terms such as *more*, *less*, *higher*, and *lower*. Be sure to complete any comparisons that start with these terms. The comparison that is started in Example 2.6.1 is not complete, forcing the reader to make an assumption about the group(s) to which the low-achieving students will be compared. The improved versions are superior because they complete the comparison that starts with the word *more*. Note that the improved versions illustrate that the comparison can be completed in more than one way, demonstrating that the original version is vague.

> ## Example 2.6.1
>
> Low-achieving primary-grade students are more dependent on adults for psychological support.
>
> ***Improved Versions of Example 2.6.1***
>
> Low-achieving primary-grade students are more dependent on adults for psychological support than are average achievers.
>
> Low-achieving primary-grade students are more dependent on adults for psychological support than are low-achieving intermediate grade students.

➤ Guideline 2.7 Because most hypotheses deal with the behavior of groups, plural forms should usually be used

In Example 2.7.1, singular terms are used to refer to the participants (e.g., "a husband," "a wife," "a partner"). Because the hypothesis will undoubtedly be tested using groups of spouses, the improved version of the hypothesis below is preferable.

Example 2.7.1

Retirement satisfaction is greater when a partner has greater marital satisfaction than when they have less marital satisfaction.

Improved Version of Example 2.7.1

Individuals who have greater marital satisfaction have greater retirement satisfaction than those with less marital satisfaction.

➤ **Guideline 2.8 Avoid gender stereotypes in the statement of a hypothesis**

In Example 2.8.1, use of the term "her level" reflects the gender stereotype that nursing is an occupation for women only. The problem has been corrected in the improved version by substituting the plural terms "nurses" and "their level." It is important to avoid gender stereotyping throughout research reports.

Example 2.8.1

There is a direct relationship between a nurse's participation in administrative decision-making and her level of job satisfaction.

Improved Version of Example 2.8.1

There is a direct relationship between nurses' participation in administrative decision-making and their level of job satisfaction.

➤ **Guideline 2.9 A hypothesis should be free of terms and phrases that do not add to its meaning**

The improved version of Example 2.9.1 is much shorter than the original version, yet its meaning is clear.

Example 2.9.1

Among elementary school teachers, those who are teaching in year-round schools have higher morale than those who are teaching in elementary schools that follow a more traditional school year schedule.

Improved Version of Example 2.9.1

Elementary school teachers who teach in year-round schools have higher morale than those who teach on a traditional schedule.

> ➤ **Guideline 2.10 A hypothesis should indicate what will be studied—not the possible implications of a study or value judgments of the author**

In Example 2.10.1, the author is expressing a value judgment rather than the anticipated relationship between the variables to be studied. The improved version indicates how religion will be treated as a variable (e.g., attendance at religious services) and indicates the specific outcome (e.g., cheating behavior) that will be studied.

Example 2.10.1

Religion is good for society.

Improved Version of Example 2.10.1

Attendance at religious services is inversely associated with students' cheating behavior while taking tests.

Note that if the hypothesis in the improved version of Example 2.10.1 is supported by the data generated to test the hypothesis, the researcher may want to assert that less cheating is "good for society" in his or her research report. Such an assertion is acceptable as long as the researcher makes it clear that the assertion is a value judgment and not a data-based conclusion.

> ➤ **Guideline 2.11 A hypothesis should name variables in the order in which they occur or will be measured**

In Example 2.11.1, the natural order has been reversed because the deprivation will precede, and possibly produce, the anticipated anxiety. This problem has been corrected in the improved version.

Example 2.11.1

More free-floating anxiety is observed among adults who are subjected to longer periods of sensory deprivation.

Improved Version of Example 2.11.1

Adults who are subjected to extended periods of sensory deprivation experience more free-floating anxiety than those exposed to less deprivation.

In Example 2.11.2, the natural order has been reversed. Because political adver-
tising precedes winning elections, advertisements should be mentioned before elec-
tion to office. The problem has been corrected in the improved version.

Example 2.11.2

Politicians who win elective offices tend to focus their political advertisements
on a limited number of issues, while those who lose elections tend to focus on
a larger number of issues.

Improved Version of Example 2.11.2

Politicians who focus their political advertisements on a limited number of
issues are more likely to win elective office than those whose advertisements
cover a larger number of issues.

The researcher would be expected to define what is meant by "limited number"
and "larger number" in the report.

➤ Guideline 2.12 Avoid using the words *significant* or *significance* in a hypothesis

The terms *significant* and *significance* usually refer to tests of statistical significance.
Because most quantitative studies include these tests, reference to them in hypotheses
is not necessary because knowledgeable readers understand that the issue of statistical
significance will be dealt with in the Results section of a quantitative research report.

Example 2.12.1 shows a hypothesis with the word *significantly* struck out because
it is not necessary (nor is it standard) to include it.

Example 2.12.1

Adults who are subjected to extended periods of sensory deprivation experience ~~significantly~~ more free-floating anxiety than those exposed to less
deprivation.

➤ Guideline 2.13 Avoid using the word *prove* in a hypothesis

Empirical research does not prove its outcomes for three primary reasons. First, empirical research is usually based only on samples from populations, and it is safe to assume that no sample is perfectly representative of any given population. Second, it is safe to assume that no test or other measurement procedure is perfectly valid and reliable. Finally, it is always possible that research has been influenced by unintentional biases. These biases can take an infinite variety of forms, such as unintentionally testing the control group in a noisier environment than the one used for testing the experimental group, or a research assistant unintentionally suggesting answers to respondents (without the researcher's knowledge) in an opinion survey. Thus, researchers should not naively set out looking for "proof" by using empirical research methods. Instead, they should recognize that they will be collecting data that offer varying degrees of confidence regarding various conclusions. The greater the degree of care taken in reducing errors, the more confidence in the results researchers are justified to have.

➤ Guideline 2.14 Avoid using two different terms to refer to the same variable in a hypothesis

In Example 2.14.1, it is not clear whether the "literature-based approach" is the same as the "new approach" because two different terms are being used. This problem has been corrected in the improved version.

Example 2.14.1

Students who receive a literature-based approach to reading instruction plus training in phonetics have better attitudes toward reading than those who receive only the new approach to reading instruction.

Improved Version of Example 2.14.1

Students who receive a literature-based approach to reading instruction plus training in phonetics have better attitudes toward reading than those who receive only the literature-based approach to reading instruction.

Note that clarity of communication is of utmost importance in scientific writing. Varying the terms used to refer to a single construct, as one might do in creative writing, is likely to impede clear scientific communication.

➤ **Guideline 2.15 Avoid making precise statistical predictions in a hypothesis**

Precise statistical predictions are rarely justified. In addition, they may make it almost impossible to confirm a hypothesis. Consider Example 2.15.1. If contamination is reduced by any percentage other than 35, the hypothesis would have to be rejected. For instance, if there is a 99% reduction in bacterial contamination, the hypothesis would need to be rejected because it is more than 35%. Likewise, if there is a 1% reduction, the hypothesis would also need to be rejected because it is less than 35%. The improved version indicates the direction of the expected relationship without naming a precise statistical outcome.

Example 2.15.1

The air of operating rooms in which the staff wear polypropylene coveralls contains 35% less bacterial contamination than in the air of operating rooms in which the staff wear conventional surgical clothing.

Improved Version of Example 2.15.1

The air of operating rooms in which the staff wear polypropylene coveralls contains less bacterial contamination than in the air of operating rooms in which the staff wear conventional surgical clothing.

➤ **Exercises for Chapter 2**

Please note that because the application of many of the guidelines in this chapter involves a certain amount of subjectivity, there may be differences of opinions on the best answers to some of the following questions.

Part A

Name the two variables in each of the following hypotheses.

1. There is an inverse relationship between ability to read and frequency of voting among elderly citizens.

2. Among college graduates, authoritarianism and anxiety are directly related.

3. Unhoused women are subjected to more spousal physical abuse than are housed women.

4. Body mass index and coronary risk are inversely related among women over 50 years of age.

5. Among first graders, there is a direct relationship between level of hand-eye coordination and achievement in tennis.

6. Among adolescents, interest in recreational reading is inversely associated with amount of time spent watching YouTube.

Part B

For each of the following hypotheses, identify the independent variable and the dependent variable. (See pages 11–13 to review these terms.)

7. Negative political advertisements are more likely to motivate citizens to vote in general elections than are positive advertisements.

8. Disruptive children who are given token rewards for remaining in their seats in a classroom setting exhibit better in-seat behavior than disruptive children who are just given verbal praise.

9. Postcardiac adults who receive telephone counseling to encourage engaging in physical exercise report walking more miles per day than postcardiac adults who do not receive telephone counseling.

Part C

For each of the following hypotheses, name the guideline(s), if any, that were not followed. Revise each hypothesis that you think contains errors. In your revisions, you may need to make some assumptions about what the authors had in mind when writing their hypotheses.

10. The hypothesis is to prove that first-born boys are more athletically competitive than are second-born boys.

11. Children differ in age, and they also differ in their ability to focus on instructional presentations.

12. The rate of development of speech in young children is directly related to the verbal fluency of their parents.

13. Among high achievers, there will be a higher level of sibling rivalry.

14. An individual who experiences marital dissatisfaction tends to be more depressed than an individual who experiences marital satisfaction.

15. Other things being equal, more rewards result in better performance.

16. The social agenda of the present administration is weak.

17. There is a direct relationship between a mechanical engineer's ability to visualize objects rotating in space and his success on the job.

18. Fifty percent of employees with poor attendance records have alcohol-related syndromes.

19. College applicants who take test preparation courses exhibit less test-taking anxiety.

20. First graders whose parents read to them on a regular basis have greater reading achievement.

21. Students who take Psychology 100 report less self-insight on a questionnaire given at the beginning of the course than on a post-test given at the end of an Introduction to Psychology course.

22. People who cheat the welfare system are unethical.

23. There will be a 25% reduction in the incidence of smoking after high school students complete a unit on the harmful effects of tobacco.

24. Using discussion groups in college sociology classes will be more effective than a traditional lecture approach to instruction.

Part D

Write a simple hypothesis on a topic of interest to you that includes an identifiable independent and dependent variable.

Your hypothesis:

Independent variable:

Dependent variable:

Part E

Write a simple hypothesis on a topic of interest to you that does not have independent and dependent variables. Mention a population in the hypothesis.

Your hypothesis:

Chapter 3

A Closer Look at Hypotheses

This chapter presents advanced guidelines for writing hypotheses and explores some of the principles from Chapter 2 in greater detail.

It is important that the research report have a coherent logical flow (guided by the research question(s)) throughout.

> ### Guideline 3.1 A single sentence may contain more than one hypothesis

It is permissible to include more than one hypothesis in a single sentence as long as the sentence is reasonably concise, and its meaning is clear.

In Example 3.1.1, there is one independent variable ("supplementary group therapy") and two anticipated outcomes or dependent variables. Therefore, there are two hypotheses: (1) Those who receive the group therapy supplement report more relief, and (2) Those who receive the group therapy supplement are more satisfied with the counseling process.

Example 3.1.1

Depressed clients whose individual counseling is supplemented with group therapy report more relief from their symptoms and greater satisfaction with the counseling process than comparable clients who receive only individual counseling.

> ### Guideline 3.2 When a number of related hypotheses are to be stated, consider presenting them in a numbered or lettered list

Example 3.2.1 shows a list of three related hypotheses.

 DOI: 10.4324/9781003230410-4

Example 3.2.1

It was hypothesized that adolescent high school students' desire to learn academic subjects is more greatly influenced by

1. same-gender peers than opposite-gender peers,
2. peers who are elected to student-body positions than those who have not been elected, and
3. peers who have excelled in non-academic areas such as sports than those who have not excelled.

A numbered list such as the one in Example 3.2.1 may be helpful when writing other sections of the research report. For instance, when discussing research results, researchers can make statements such as the ones shown in Examples 3.2.2 and 3.2.3. Notice that numbering the hypotheses early in a research report makes it easier to refer clearly to a specific hypothesis without having to restate the entire hypothesis. In Example 3.2.2, this was done with a parenthetical phrase. In Example 3.2.3, there is no parenthetical phrase. Either form is correct; however, many copy editors discourage the overuse of parentheses.

Example 3.2.2

Regarding the first hypothesis (same- versus opposite-gender influence), the results are clear. The mean score for the …

Example 3.2.3

The results are clear regarding the influence of same- versus opposite-gender peers specified in Hypothesis Number 1. The mean score for the …

➤ **Guideline 3.3 The hypothesis or hypotheses should be stated before the Method section**

The Method section of a research report describes how the researcher tested the hypothesis. Therefore, the hypothesis should be stated before describing the methods used to test the hypothesis.

In journal articles, hypotheses are usually stated in the final paragraphs of the literature review, which serves as an introduction in the research report. Immediately following the literature review is the Method section. (See Example 1.4.1 in Chapter 1 to review the structure of a basic research report.)

In theses and dissertations, the hypotheses are usually stated at the end of the first chapter/introduction. The second chapter is usually the literature review. The hypotheses may be stated again at the end of the second chapter because the hypotheses should flow logically from the literature that has been reviewed.

➤ Guideline 3.4 While some researchers use alternative terms, the term *hypothesis* is preferred

Some researchers begin the statements of their hypotheses with terms such as *predicted*, *speculated*, and *expected* in phrases such as the one in Example 3.4.1. While this is acceptable, it is best to use the formal term *hypothesis* or *hypothesized* instead of alternative terms. This is illustrated in Example 3.4.1 and its improved version.

Example 3.4.1

Based on prior research, it was expected that low-income women who are subjected to domestic abuse are at greater risk for being unemployed than low-income women who are not subjected to domestic abuse.

Improved Version of Example 3.4.1

Based on prior research, it was hypothesized that low-income women who are subjected to domestic abuse are at greater risk for being unemployed than low-income women who are not subjected to domestic abuse.

➤ Guideline 3.5 In a research report, a hypothesis should flow from the narrative that immediately precedes it

A research report typically begins with a literature review, which serves as the introduction to the report. Typically, the hypothesis is stated at the end of the literature review.

There should be a clear, logical connection between the findings in the literature and the researcher's hypothesis. In Example 3.5.1, the researcher explicitly reminds readers of the main thrust of the findings in the literature in order to demonstrate that the hypothesis flows from the literature (i.e., it is logically based on the findings in the literature).

Example 3.5.1

The preceding literature review clearly indicates that teachers in the Salilii tribe rely more heavily on physical punishment than on rewards for maintaining discipline among children in the classroom. The literature also indicates a large number of cultural parallels between the Salilii tribe and the Lani tribe. Thus, it was hypothesized that teachers in the Lani tribe also rely more heavily on physical punishment than on rewards for maintaining discipline.

➤ **Guideline 3.6 Both directional and nondirectional hypotheses are acceptable**

Up to this point, all the hypotheses in this book have been directional. A *directional* hypothesis indicates the direction of the difference expected. For instance, in Example 3.6.1, the direction of the difference is clearly stated (e.g., low-socioeconomic status is associated with more authoritarianism). In contrast, Example 3.6.2 is *nondirectional* because it predicts that a difference will be found but does not indicate the direction of the difference.

Example 3.6.1

Directional hypothesis: It is hypothesized that police officers reared in low-socioeconomic status (SES) families are more authoritarian than police officers reared in middle–SES families.

Example 3.6.2

Nondirectional hypothesis: Police officers reared in low-socioeconomic status families differ in their level of authoritarianism from police officers reared in middle-socioeconomic status families.

Example 3.6.3 shows a directional hypothesis for an experimental study (e.g., a study in which treatments will be administered in order to see if they cause changes in the participants). It predicts that one group will report a lower level of pain than the other. In contrast, Example 3.6.4 shows a corresponding nondirectional hypothesis, which predicts only that the two groups will differ in their reports of pain. It does not predict which group will report less pain.

Example 3.6.3

Directional hypothesis: It is hypothesized that adult males with Condition X who are administered Drug A report a lower level of pain than a comparable group of adult males who are administered Drug B.

Example 3.6.4

Nondirectional hypothesis: It is hypothesized that adult males with Condition X who are administered Drug A report a different level of pain than a comparable group of adult males who are administered Drug B.

When researchers have a basis for predicting the outcome of a study, they should state a directional hypothesis. When they do not have such a basis, they should state a nondirectional one.

Note that directional hypotheses are much more frequently used as the basis for research than nondirectional hypotheses. One reason for this is the expectation of specific kinds of differences usually motivates researchers to conduct research.

> **Guideline 3.7 When a researcher has a research hypothesis, it should be stated; the null hypothesis need not always be stated**

A *research hypothesis* is the hypothesis that a researcher believes will be supported by their data. When a researcher has such a hypothesis (whether it is directional or nondirectional; see the previous guideline), it should be stated in the research report.

In contrast, the *null hypothesis* is a statistical hypothesis that states that a difference is attributable to random errors created by random sampling. For instance, if a random sample is designated as an experimental group and is administered a new drug while another random sample is selected to be the control group, a difference at the end of the experiment might be attributable to inequalities between the two groups created by the random selection (e.g., quite at random, one group might be more predisposed to improve than the other).

In other words, the null hypothesis states that there is no true difference—only a random one. Significance tests are used to test the null hypothesis. (Students who have not taken a statistics course should consult Appendix C for an introduction to the null hypothesis and significance testing.)

In journal articles, formal statements of null hypotheses are almost always omitted because they always have the same content—regardless of how they are worded (e.g., they always attribute any differences to random errors). Thus, it would be redundant to repeat the null hypothesis in all quantitative research reports.

In term projects, theses, and dissertations, however, students are sometimes required to state null hypotheses in order to demonstrate that they understand the purpose of the significance tests that they have conducted. (The purpose of a significance test is to test the null hypothesis.) Examples 3.7.1 and 3.7.2 illustrate some ways that the null hypothesis can be stated. Because there is more than one way to word a null hypothesis, two statements are shown in each example. Only one statement, however, should be used in a research report.

Example 3.7.1

Research hypothesis: The research hypothesis is that social standing in campus organizations is directly related to friendliness.

One version of the corresponding null hypothesis: The null hypothesis is that there is no true relationship between social standing in campus organizations and friendliness.

Another version of the corresponding null hypothesis: The null hypothesis is that the relationship between social standing in campus organizations and friendliness is non-existent in the population from which the sample was drawn.

Example 3.7.2

Research hypothesis: The research hypothesis is that private school graduates have a higher proportion of parents in high-status occupations than public school graduates.

One version of the corresponding null hypothesis: The null hypothesis is that there is no true difference in the proportion of parents in high-status occupations between the populations of private school and public school graduates.

Another version of the corresponding null hypothesis: The null hypothesis is that the observed difference between the proportions of parents in high-status occupations for private school graduates and public school graduates is the result of chance variations associated with the random sampling process.

Exercises for Chapter 3

Please note that because the application of many of the guidelines in this chapter involves a certain amount of subjectivity, there may be differences of opinions on the best answers to some of the following questions.

Part A

Answer the questions based on the guidelines presented within this chapter.

1. Is it permissible to include more than one hypothesis in a single sentence? Explain.

2. Very briefly explain why it may be helpful to present a numbered (or lettered) list of hypotheses when more than one hypothesis will be examined in a single research study.

3. Where are hypotheses usually stated in journal articles?

4. Where are hypotheses usually stated in theses and dissertations?

5. According to this chapter, how could the following statement be improved? "Based on the literature reviewed above, it was predicted that politicians who emphasize position X are viewed more favorably by the electorate than politicians who emphasize position Y."

6. Rewrite the following directional hypothesis to make it nondirectional. "Elementary school students taught reading with the XYZ method obtain higher reading comprehension test scores than those taught with the ABC method."

7. Write a null hypothesis that corresponds to the following research hypothesis. "It is hypothesized that there is a direct relationship between the extent to which social workers empathize with their clients and the clients' rate of compliance with the X rule."

Part B

8. Write a directional hypothesis on a topic of interest to you. Then write a corresponding null hypothesis for it.

9. Rewrite the directional hypothesis that you wrote for Question 8 to make it nondirectional.

Part C

10. If you will be writing a thesis or dissertation, examine theses or dissertations using your college/university library online catalog. Do any of the examples you found contain statements of the null hypothesis? Be sure to take note of any links to examples that contain null hypotheses.

Chapter 4

Writing Research Objectives and Questions

The previous two chapters cover writing research hypotheses, which indicate the predicted relationship among two or more variables.[1] This chapter covers two alternatives to hypotheses: research objectives (also called research purposes) and research questions.

> ## Guideline 4.1 When no relationship will be examined, consider stating a research objective

In Example 4.1.1, no relationships are being examined. Instead, the researchers want to determine only one thing—"public support levels." Thus, it would be inappropriate to try to state it as a hypothesis. A statement of the *objective* is appropriate.

Example 4.1.1

The research objective was to determine public support levels for the bond measure to fund the construction of additional public libraries.[2]

Likewise, no relationship is implied in Example 4.1.2. Instead, the researchers want to determine only what is being done to provide "practical training on ethical issues ..."

Example 4.1.2

The objective of our research was to determine what traditional graduate training programs in nursing were doing to provide practical training on ethical issues regarding euthanasia.

➤ Guideline 4.2 When no relationship will be examined, consider posing a research question

An alternative to a research objective is a research question. The most basic form of a research question is to ask whether there is a relationship between two or more variables. The literature may not always be robust enough to allow for a statement of a hypothesis, but a research question can always be posed. Example 4.2.1 shows the most basic form of a research question. Examples 4.2.2 and 4.2.3 show research objectives restated as research questions.

Example 4.2.1

What is the relationship between peer pressure and childhood anxiety?

Example 4.2.2

The research *objective* was to determine public support levels for the bond measure to fund the construction of additional public libraries.

The research *question* was as follows: What is the level of public support for the bond measure that will provide funding for the construction of additional public libraries?

Example 4.2.3

The *objective* of our research was to determine what traditional graduate training programs in nursing were doing to provide practical training on ethical issues regarding euthanasia.

The research *question* was as follows: What are traditional graduate training programs in nursing doing to provide practical training on ethical issues regarding euthanasia?

➤ Guideline 4.3 Stating a research objective or posing a research question are equally acceptable

The choice between stating a research objective or a research question is a matter of choosing the form that reads more smoothly in a particular context. One form is not inherently preferable to the other.

➤ **Guideline 4.4 Avoid writing a research question that implies that the answer will be a simple "yes" or "no"**

Example 4.4.1 violates this guideline. Most research is based on complex concepts, and the results are usually not simple. Yet Example 4.4.1 implies that the researchers are interested only in a "yes" or "no" answer. The improved version poses a more realistic question.

Example 4.4.1

Research Question: Do adolescents believe that their peers have favorable views of marijuana?

Improved Version of Example 4.4.1

Research Question: To what extent do adolescents believe that their peers have favorable views of marijuana?

Compare Example 4.4.2 and its improved version. Research on complex human behavior such as reading achievement seldom yields a simple "yes" or "no" answer. Hence, the improved version is superior.

Example 4.4.2

Research Question: In the long run, does a literature-based approach produce higher levels of overall reading achievement than a phonics-based approach?

Improved Version of Example 4.4.2

Research Question: In the long run, what are the relative contributions of literature-based and phonics-based approaches to overall reading achievement?

Of course, the terms "long run," "literature-based [approach]," and "phonics-based [approach]" will need to be defined in the research report. Writing definitions in research is covered in Chapter 7.

➤ **Guideline 4.5 When previous research is contradictory, consider using a research objective or a research question instead of a hypothesis**

Sometimes researchers are unwilling to make a prediction because the previous research on the topic has had contradictory findings. Such contradictions can occur for a variety of reasons, such as different researchers using different types of samples and measures in various studies as well as using different definitions of the variables studied. In such a situation, it may be more appropriate to state a research objective or question instead of a hypothesis.

> ➤ **Guideline 4.6 When a new topic is to be examined, consider using a research objective or a research question instead of a hypothesis**

Researchers sometimes identify new problems for research. For instance, prior to the COVID-19 pandemic there had been no research on the psychological effects of pandemics on children in the United States. In light of the lack of previous research, it may have been more appropriate to state a research question (or objective) instead of a hypothesis, as is done in Example 4.6.1.

Example 4.6.1

Research Question: What was the nature and extent of the psychological impact of the COVID-19 pandemic on middle-school children residing in the greater New York City metropolitan area?

Example 4.6.1 could be rewritten as a research objective without changing the meaning of the researcher's question, as illustrated in Example 4.6.2.

Example 4.6.2

Research Objective: To explore the nature and extent of the psychological impact of the COVID-19 pandemic on middle-school children residing in the greater New York City metropolitan area.

> ➤ **Guideline 4.7 For *qualitative* research, consider writing a research objective or question instead of a hypothesis**

Most qualitative researchers approach their research topics without imposing hypotheses derived from theory or previous research. Instead, they attempt to *follow the data* (e.g., as they analyze the data, they attempt to identify themes and relationships based on participants' responses).

Nevertheless, qualitative researchers need to state one or more research objectives or questions at the onset of their study, even if the objective or question is less specific than the ones posed by quantitative researchers.

Example 4.7.1 shows the research question for a qualitative study, and Example 4.7.2 shows a research purpose (i.e., research objective). These illustrate the degree of specificity desirable in research questions and objectives for qualitative research. Note that these statements were made in the last paragraph of the literature review, which serves as the introduction to the research. This is the same place in which quantitative researchers state their hypotheses, questions, and objectives.

Example 4.7.1

The central research question driving the investigation was expressed as, "How do students with a mental health disability describe their learning barriers when studying through online education?"[3]

Example 4.7.2

The purpose of the study was to examine the impacts of course activities on student perceptions of engagement and learning in online courses.[4]

> ### Guideline 4.8 A research objective or question should be as specific as possible yet be comprehensible

The need for specificity in hypotheses is discussed under Guideline 2.5 in Chapter 2. Application of this guideline is often problematic. Consider, for instance, Example 4.8.1. It is quite specific, actually naming two specific instruments (i.e., measuring tools). However, for readers who are not familiar with the specific instruments (i.e., the scale and the inventory), the research objective may be too specific.[5] Thus, writers must judge whether their audiences are likely to be familiar with the specific item(s) mentioned—in this case, the specific instruments.

For readers who are not familiar with the specific scale and inventory in Example 4.8.1, the improved version is superior. Of course, readers of the research report will expect to learn later in the report how the two variables were measured.

Example 4.8.1

The objective was to determine the extent to which college students' scores on the Voloskovoy Self-Esteem Scale correlate with scores on the Smith-Doe Cultural Tolerance Inventory.

Improved Version of Example 4.8.1

The objective was to determine the extent to which college students' self-esteem correlates with their tolerance of cultural differences.

➤ **Guideline 4.9 When stating related objectives or questions, consider presenting them in a numbered or lettered list**

In Example 4.9.1, the researchers present a numbered list of questions.

Example 4.9.1

RQ 1. What challenges do students and parents face with distance learning, and how do they cope with them?

RQ 2. How do individual characteristics (academic achievement, motivational-affective prerequisites, age group, and gender) relate to students' self-perceived coping success?

RQ 3. What effect does school, family, and peer support have on students' self-perceived coping success?[6]

The numbered list in Example 4.9.1 allows the researchers to refer to individual research questions by number later in the report. For instance, in the Results section, a researcher might say, "The results for research question 1 clearly indicate that …" and later make a statement such as "For research question 2, the results suggest that …"

In Example 4.9.2, the researchers start with a general, overarching research question followed by a lettered list of the specific questions on which data were collected. This arrangement is usually desirable when there are a number of related research questions that were investigated.

Example 4.9.2

This study examined the following general research question: How do teachers who leave their profession before retirement age arrive at their decision?

The more specific research questions included (a) With whom did they discuss their impending decision? (b) What resources did they consult? (c) How long did they consider the impending decision before finalizing it? and (d) How did they carry out their decision?

➢ **Guideline 4.10 A research objective or question should flow from the literature review that immediately precedes it**

Research reports typically begin with a literature review, which serves as the introduction to the report. The literature review should logically lead readers to the research objectives or questions (or hypotheses)—that is, the rationale for formulating the objectives or questions should be made clear by the literature review.

Example 4.10.1 shows the final sentence of the last paragraph of a literature review on contextual contexts for children's and adolescents' coping with learning during the COVID-19 pandemic. The research questions that follow the paragraph flow directly from it.

Example 4.10.1

Therefore, limited attention has been given to the mechanisms through which peers affect outcomes.

The current mixed-methods study examines the variance in students' learning in times of COVID-19 concerning characteristics and contextual resources within their school, family, and peer context. Therefore, this study addresses three research questions:

RQ 1. What challenges do students and parents face with distance learning, and how do they cope with them?

RQ 2. How do individual characteristics (academic achievement, motivational-affective prerequisites, age group, and gender) relate to students' self-perceived coping success?

RQ 3. What effect does school, family, and peer support have on students' self-perceived coping success?[7]

Exercises for Chapter 4

Part A

1. Rewrite the following research question as a research objective: "To what extent do primary care physicians and specialists inquire about patients' lifestyle characteristics that may affect patients' overall health?"

2. Rewrite this research objective as a research question: "The objective of this research is to estimate the extent to which religious affiliation predicts voter sentiment regarding bond measures for public schools."

3. According to this chapter, is stating a research question inherently better than stating a research objective? Why or why not?

4. Which of the guidelines in this chapter is clearly violated in the following research question? "Is the Internet useful for teaching psychology?"

5. "When previous research is contradictory, stating a research hypothesis rather than an objective or question is clearly preferable." Is this statement true *or* false?

6. For which of the following types of research would stating a research hypothesis be less likely?

   A. Qualitative research
   B. Quantitative research

7. Which of the guidelines in this chapter is violated by the following research objective? "The objective is to determine whether the use of the Barnes Advocacy Teaching Method results in higher scores on the Dobrowsky Scale of International Understanding."

8. Which of the following arrangements is recommended in this chapter?

   A. Present a literature review that flows from the research objective or question that is stated first.
   B. Present a research objective or question that flows from the literature review that immediately precedes it.

Part B

9. Write a research objective on a topic of interest to you. Then rewrite it as a research question. Which form (objective or question) do you prefer? Why?

Part C

10. Review three journal articles, theses, or dissertations that contain statements of research objectives or questions, and make note of the following:

    A. In how many cases are the research objectives or questions presented in the last paragraph before the section on methods (i.e., at the end of the literature review)?

    B. In articles that contain more than one objective or question, are the objectives or questions presented as a numbered (or lettered) list?

Notes

1 A relationship can take two forms: (a) an *association*, such as higher levels of depression are associated with lower levels of self-esteem, and (b) a *difference*, such as those who receive group counseling will be less depressed than those who receive individual counseling.
2 For a research *proposal*, always use the present tense (e.g., "The research objective *is* to determine …").
3 McManus et al. (2017, p. 338).
4 Tsai et al. (2021, p. 106).
5 Instruments such as attitude scales and inventories need to be described in detail in the section of the research report on methods. This topic is covered in Chapter 9.
6 Simm et al. (2021, p. 5).
7 Ibid. (pp. 4–5).

Chapter 5

Writing Titles

Because titles perform the important function of helping consumers of research identify research reports that are of interest to them, they should be written with considerable care.

➢ **Guideline 5.1 If only a small number of variables are studied, the title should name the variables**

In Example 5.1.1, there are two variables: (1) self-esteem and (2) aggressiveness.

Example 5.1.1

The Relationship between Self-Esteem and Aggressiveness.

In Example 5.1.2, there is one variable: attitudes toward vaping.

Example 5.1.2

Adolescents' Attitudes toward Vaping.

➢ **Guideline 5.2 A title should not be a complete sentence**

Notice that Examples 5.1.1 and 5.1.2 are not sentences and do not end with a period, both of which are appropriate characteristics of titles.

➢ **Guideline 5.3 If many variables are studied, only the *types* of variables should be named**

Suppose a researcher examined how students' attitudes toward school change over time with attention to differences among urban, suburban, and rural groups, various

 DOI: 10.4324/9781003230410-6

socioeconomic groups, gender, and so on. Because there are too many variables to name in a concise title, only the main variable(s) should be specifically named, while the others may be referred to by type, as illustrated in Example 5.3.1. In this example, the main variable of "attitudes toward school" is mentioned, while the term "demographic variables" is used to stand for a variety of background variables such as socioeconomic status and gender.

Example 5.3.1

Relationships between Students' Attitudes toward School and Selected Demographic Variables.

> **Guideline 5.4 The title of a journal article should be concise; the title of a thesis or dissertation may be longer**

Titles of journal articles tend to be concise. A simple survey that we conducted illustrates this point. A count of the number of words in the titles of a random sample of 152 research articles on mathematics education that appeared in 42 journals in a recent year revealed that the median (average) number of words was close to 11. Example 5.4.1 is the shortest one identified in the survey. It is exceptionally short and could be improved by incorporating a reference to the variables studied.

Example 5.4.1

The Mathematics Department.

Example 5.4.2 is the longest title identified in the survey. It is long only because the specific countries are listed. If it ended with "in Various Countries" instead of with the list, it would be more concise but less descriptive. If the research report was for dissemination in the United States, an alternative would be to end the title with "… in the United States and Other Countries."

Example 5.4.2

Grade Placement of Addition and Subtraction Topics in Japan, Mainland China, the Soviet Union, Taiwan, and the United States.

Example 5.4.3 shows a title of about average length for the sample of titles examined. It illustrates Guideline 5.4 because the types of variables, "personality factors" and "biographical factors," are referred to, while the specific personality traits and types of biographical data collected are not specifically named.

Example 5.4.3

Contributions of Some Personality and Biographical Factors to Mathematical Creativity.

For a random sample of titles of dissertations on mathematics education during the same recent year, the average number of words in the titles was almost 19, which is considerably more than the average of 11 for journal articles. A variation on the longest dissertation title is shown in Example 5.4.4.

Example 5.4.4

A Descriptive Study of Verbal Problems in Mathematics Textbooks for Grades Seven and Eight from Four Decades: the 1970s, the 1980s, the 1990s, and the 2000s.

Students who are preparing theses or dissertations should ask their committees whether concise titles—such as those commonly used in journals—or longer titles—which are more typical (but not universal) in theses and dissertations—are expected. If a shorter title is desired, the shortened version shown immediately below illustrates how this could be done.

Shortened Version of the Title in Example 5.4.4

Verbal Problems in Mathematics Textbooks for Grades Seven and Eight: 1970–2010.

➤ **Guideline 5.5 A title should indicate what was studied— not the findings of the study**

All the previous examples illustrate this guideline. Example 5.5.1 violates the guideline because it states the finding that "food and alcohol disturbance is associated." This is corrected in the improved version by omitting the result. Also, note that the original version is a complete sentence, which violates Guideline 5.2.

Example 5.5.1

Food and Alcohol Disturbance Is Associated with Sorority Affiliation.

Improved Version of Example 5.5.1

A Comparison of Food and Alcohol Disturbance (FAD) in Sorority and Non-Sorority Women.[1]

Guideline 5.5 may surprise some beginning students of empirical methods because results and conclusions are often stated in titles in the media. This is the case because the media frequently reports straightforward facts. "Five Die in Downtown Hotel Fire" is a perfectly acceptable title for a factual article of limited scope. Because empirical research reports are likely to raise as many questions as they resolve, a title that states a simple factual result or conclusion is usually inappropriate.

➤ Guideline 5.6 Consider mentioning the population(s) in a title

This guideline is especially applicable when a study has been deliberately delimited to a particular population. In Example 5.6.1, the population is delimited to California farm workers.

Example 5.6.1

Coccidioidomycosis Knowledge and Behaviors of California Hispanic Farm Workers.[2]

In Example 5.6.2, the title indicates that the population consists of older Hispanic populations. Such information helps consumers of research identify articles on populations of interest to them.

Example 5.6.2

Influenza and Pneumococcal Vaccination Delivery in Older Hispanic Populations in the United States.[3]

Note that sometimes a particular type of participant is studied only because that type is readily available to a researcher. For instance, a researcher might conduct a study on a theory of learning using students enrolled in his or her introductory psychology class (because they are readily available) even though the researcher is interested in the application of the theory to students in general. In such a case, mention of the type of population in the title is less important than when a researcher deliberately selects participants from a particular population of special interest.

➤ Guideline 5.7 Consider the use of subtitles to indicate the methods of study

While it is not necessary to mention the methods used to conduct a study (e.g., a survey, an experiment, and so on), this information can be helpful for consumers of research trying to identify particular types of studies. However, when initially trying to locate research reports on a given topic, most consumers are more interested in the variables studied (and the populations) than in the method(s) used to conduct the studies. This suggests that it is best to name variables and populations in the main title, followed by a subtitle indicating the method used to conduct the study. This is illustrated in the improved versions of Examples 5.7.1 and 5.7.2.

Example 5.7.1

A Pilot Study on the Role of Alcoholism in Dysfunctional Families

Improved Version of Example 5.7.1

The Role of Alcoholism in Dysfunctional Families: A Pilot Study.

Example 5.7.2

A National Survey of Experienced Kindergarten Teachers' Definitions of Literacy.

Improved Version of Example 5.7.2

Experienced Kindergarten Teachers' Definitions of Literacy: A National Survey.

➤ Guideline 5.8 If a study is strongly tied to a particular model or theory, consider mentioning it in the title

Some consumers of research are especially interested in studies that shed light on particular models or theories. If a study was designed to explore some aspect of these, mentioning this in the title will help consumers locate relevant research. In Example 5.8.1, a theory is mentioned in the subtitle, while a theory is mentioned in the main title of Example 5.8.2. While either placement is acceptable, note that Example 5.8.2 places more emphasis on the theory than does Example 5.8.1.

Example 5.8.1

The Role of Male Siblings in the Mathematics Achievement of Adolescent Girls: A Social Learning Theory Perspective.

Example 5.8.2

Application of the Theory of Planned Behavior in the Treatment of Adolescents with Multi-Drug Dependence Issues.

➤ **Guideline 5.9 Omit the names of specific measures unless they are the focus of the research**

Mentioning specific measures in titles can make them unnecessarily long without providing key information to consumers of research. Example 5.9.1 shows a title that has been made unnecessarily long by naming a specific instrument. Compare it with the improved version.

Example 5.9.1

The Effectiveness of a Home Care Program for Improving the Functional Abilities of Elderly Individuals as Measured by the Functional Abilities Self-Rating Scale.

Improved Version of Example 5.9.1

The Effectiveness of a Home Care Program for Improving the Functional Abilities of Elderly Individuals.

One reason that it is not necessary to include specific measures is that researchers interested in locating published articles that utilize specific measures or theories will narrow their database queries with those particulars in mind.

The main exception to this guideline is when the instruments are the focus of the research, such as research on the reliability and validity of specific instruments. Example 5.9.2 shows a title in which it is appropriate to name a specific instrument.

Example 5.9.2

Development of the Grandparents' Role Identity Scale: A Reliability and Validity Study.

➤ **Guideline 5.10 A title may be in the form of a question, but this form should be used sparingly and with caution**

Questions, when used as titles, are less formal than titles expressed in the form of statements. Thus, questions as titles are sometimes preferred in less formal types of publications such as workshop materials.

When using a question as a title for a research report, avoid stating it as a question that implies that it can be answered with a simple "yes" or "no." Notice that the title in Example 5.10.1 implies that the result will be a simple "yes" or "no" answer, which is seldom the case in empirical research because empirical methods yield varying degrees of confidence in results—not final answers. In the first improved version of Example 5.10.1, the problem has been fixed by posing the question in such a way that it cannot be answered with a simple "yes" or "no." The second improved version of Example 5.10.1 shows that the problem can be avoided by using a statement instead of a question.

Example 5.10.1

Do Private Colleges and Universities Accommodate Students with Physical Disabilities?

First Improved Version of Example 5.10.1

To What Extent Do Private Colleges and Universities Accommodate Students with Physical Disabilities?

Second Improved Version of Example 5.10.1

Private Colleges and Universities' Accommodations of Students with Physical Disabilities.

➤ **Guideline 5.11 In titles, use the words *effect* and *influence* with caution**

The words *effect* and *influence* are frequently used in the titles of research reports in which cause-and-effect relationships were studied. To examine such relationships, true experimental, quasi-experimental, or rigorous ex post facto methods should usually be employed. As a general rule, only reports on these methods should contain these words in their titles.

Examples 5.11.1 and 5.11.2 illustrate the appropriate use of the word *effect* in titles of reports on experiments. The typical form is as follows: "The effect(s) of an independent variable (treatment or stimulus) on a dependent variable (outcome or response)."

Example 5.11.1

The Effects of Three Schedules of Reinforcement on the Maze Performance of Rats.

Example 5.11.2

The Effects of Using App-Based Technology on Achievement on a Standardized Test of Writing Skills.

Note that *effects* is used as a noun in the two examples. As a noun, it means "influence." When used as a noun, the word *affect* means "feelings or emotions." Clearly, *effect* is the correct noun to use in these examples.

> **Guideline 5.12 A title should be consistent with the research hypothesis, objective, purpose, or question**

In Examples 5.12.1 and 5.12.2, research purposes are stated. The corresponding titles closely mirror the statements of purpose.

Example 5.12.1

Research Purpose: The purpose of this research was to explore the personal, emotional and pedagogical experiences of undergraduate students who have chosen to take a module about death and dying at university.

Corresponding Title: Teaching Death to Undergraduates: Exploring the Student Experience of Discussing Emotive Topics in the University Classroom.[4]

Example 5.12.2

Research Purpose: The purpose of this investigation was to determine the utility of a peer teaching mentor to graduate teaching assistants.

Corresponding Title: Utility of a Peer Teaching Mentor to Graduate Teaching Assistants.[5]

➤ **Guideline 5.13 Consider mentioning unique features of a study in its title**

Suppose a researcher conducted the first long-term follow-up study on the effects of a drug. The researcher would be wise to indicate in the title that the study is a long-term one, as shown in Example 5.13.1.

Example 5.13.1

The Long-Term Effects of Tetracycline on Tooth Enamel Erosion.

➤ **Guideline 5.14 Avoid using "clever" titles**

In Example 5.14.1, only the phrase "Publishing Criminal Justice Research" is informative. The reader will assume that an article deals with contemporary issues unless the title indicates that the study is historical. Thus, reference to the new millennium is not needed. The subtitle is completely uninformative and appears to have been written in an effort to be clever.

Example 5.14.1

Publishing Criminal Justice Research in the New Millennium: Things Gutenberg Never Taught You.

In Example 5.14.2, "Taking the Sting Out of Stuttering" is a rhetorical phrase that does not contribute to the readers' understanding of the topic of the research. The phrase should be omitted.

Example 5.14.2

Taking the Sting Out of Stuttering: A Comparison of the Effectiveness of Two Methods for Treating Stuttering.

In general, throughout research reports, avoid the temptation to be clever or humorous. The function of a research report is to inform—not to entertain.

➤ **Guideline 5.15 Learn the conventions for capitalization in titles**

In APA style, titles at the beginning of research reports follow the usual rules of capitalization for titles as illustrated in all the titles in this chapter. However, in a reference list, only three elements are capitalized: (1) the first letter of the first word, (2) the first letter of the first word in a subtitle, and (3) proper nouns. This is illustrated in all the references in the reference list near the end of this book.

Exercises for Chapter 5

Part A

1. When should the types of variables (instead of the individual variables) be mentioned in a title?

2. Do the titles of journal articles tend to be longer than the titles of theses and dissertations?

3. Why should a researcher avoid stating the findings of a study in the title?

4. According to this chapter, which are more formal as titles: "statements" *or* "questions"?

5. Which of the following titles is correct?

    A. The Affects of Treatment A on Outcome B

    B. The Effects of Treatment A on Outcome B

Part B

Comment on the adequacy of each of the following titles for research articles.

6. Child Care Subsidies Increase the Number of Mothers Who Are Employed Full-Time

7. Watering the Proverbial Garden: Effective Communication between Teachers and School Administrators

8. The Political Scientist

9. Are Age and Tenure Related to the Job Satisfaction of Social Workers?

10. Can Economists Predict Recessions?

11. The Effects of Peer Coaching on Achievement in English, Mathematics, History, Foreign Language, Geography, and Physics among Tenth-, Eleventh-, and Twelfth-Graders: An Experiment Conducted in Five Major Urban Areas during the 2009–2010 School Year Using Multiple Measures of Achievement with Analyses by Gender and Grade Level

12. Forbidden Fruit Tastes Especially Sweet: A Study of Lawyers' Ethical Behavior

13. The Out-Migration from Southern California Is Driven by High Housing Costs

14. Self-Monitoring by Employees Increases the Productivity of Online Workers

Part C

Write a title that you think would be appropriate for a research report that has this research objective: "The objective of this research was to explore the effects of peer mentoring on academic success in first-generation college students."

Part D

Write a research objective or hypothesis on a topic of interest to you. Once complete, write an appropriate title.

Notes

1 Rancourt et al. (2022, p. 30).
2 Sipan et al. (2022, p. 197).
3 Heintzman (2022, p. 854).
4 Pitimson (2021, p. 470).
5 Joyce & Hassenfeldt (2020, p. 12).

Chapter 6

Writing Introductions and Literature Reviews

The purpose of an introduction and literature review in an empirical research report is to introduce the problem area, establish its importance, and establish the context for the current study.

The guidelines that follow apply to all types of empirical research reports, except where noted.

➤ **Guideline 6.1 In theses and dissertations, the first chapter is usually an introduction**

The introduction in a thesis or dissertation should start by indicating the problem area and the importance of the problem, followed by a summary of the approach that will be used to investigate the problem. Typically, the introductory chapter concludes with a statement of the research hypotheses, objectives, or questions that underlie the study being reported on.

Usually, there are relatively few references to literature in this chapter because a comprehensive literature review is presented in the second chapter. However, it is acceptable to refer to some highlights of the literature review with statements such as, "As will be shown in the next chapter, the majority of surveys on this topic have revealed ..."

➤ **Guideline 6.2 In theses and dissertations, the second chapter presents a comprehensive literature review**

Students who are preparing theses and dissertations are typically expected to present comprehensive literature reviews in the second chapter. These reviews are usually much more comprehensive than those in other research reports, such as reports in journals and reports for term projects.

DOI: 10.4324/9781003230410-7

The requirement for a comprehensive literature review stems from the fact that a thesis or dissertation is, in effect, a test (i.e., an extended take-home examination) in which students are to demonstrate their ability to identify all literature of relevance to a topic and to synthesize it (i.e., evaluate and present the literature in a way that helps make sense of the individual pieces).

The research hypotheses, objectives, or questions might be restated at the end of the literature review chapter.

➤ **Guideline 6.3 In most research reports, literature reviews serve as the introduction to the reports**

In reports, such as those in journals and those prepared for term projects, the literature review typically is used to introduce the topic of the research. In other words, instead of starting with an introduction that presents the writers' personal views on the problem, writers cite literature to introduce the problem.

Example 6.3.1 shows the first paragraph of a literature review in which the topic of graduate student mentoring programs is introduced with citations to literature on the topic.

Example 6.3.1

The predominant purpose of the graduate student-faculty mentor relationship is to accomplish goals and achieve academic growth for the mentee (Brill et al., 2014). Mentors can help graduate students accomplish their goals by guiding them into the academic community and helping them to develop a professional network (Kumar et al., 2013; Yob & Crawford, 2012). Starting at the department level, mentors can be instrumental in helping to socialize students into the academic world (O'Meara et al., 2013). Faculty mentors are largely accepted as an influence on what graduate students learn, including aspects such as departmental rules and understanding of the family science field (Barnes et al., 2012). Across fields, graduate students report strong mentoring and a positive mentor-mentee relationship to be essential for academic success (O'Meara et al., 2013), a sentiment that is echoed by family science graduate students (Koblinsky et al., 2006).[1]

➤ **Guideline 6.4 In most research reports, literature reviews are selective**

In reports other than theses and dissertations, literature reviews are selective, including references only to the most relevant literature. The literature review needs to be only long enough to bring the reader up to date regarding current thinking on, and knowledge of, a problem and to establish the context for the current research.

➤ **Guideline 6.5 A literature review should be an essay—
      not a list of annotations**

An annotation is a brief summary. A list of annotations indicates what research is available on a topic but fails to organize the material for the reader. Specifically, a list of annotations fails to indicate how the individual citations relate to one another and what trends the writer has observed in the published literature.

To implement this guideline, it is best to begin by preparing a topic outline such as the one in Example 6.5.1 to guide in writing a literature review. When writing the review based on such an outline, the temptation to string together a set of annotations will be minimized.

Example 6.5.1

Topic Outline for a Literature Review

1. Importance of question-asking by children
   a. As a skill used in learning in school
   b. As a functional skill in the home and other non-school settings

2. Introduction to two basic types of questions
   a. Request for factual information (who, what, and when)
   b. Questions about causation (why)
   c. Functions of the two types in school

3. Relationship between parents' and children's verbal behavior
   a. On other verbal variables
   b. On question-asking behavior: quantity and type

4. Relationship between culture and verbal behavior
   a. Examples of how and why cultures may vary in their question-asking behavior
   b. Functions of questions in target cultures

5. Statement of the research objectives
   a. Determine types and numbers of questions asked by children in a structured learning environment
   b. Determine the relationship between question-asking by children and by parents, with attention to both number and type
   c. Determine differences in question-asking behavior among target cultures

---

> **Guideline 6.6 A literature review should lead logically to research hypotheses, objectives, or questions**

After having read a literature review, readers should understand why the researcher has formulated the specific hypotheses, objectives, or questions that underlie the research being reported. For instance, the current research might be designed to (1) extend the prior research into new areas or with new populations, (2) improve on the prior research in terms of the research methods used, or (3) test some tenet of a theory described in the literature review.

Note that new topics that are unrelated to any existing literature are exceedingly rare. Progress in science is usually based on researchers building on the previous work of other researchers. A literature review should show this progression, especially the progression from the existing literature to the current study.

> **Guideline 6.7 Research hypotheses, objectives, or questions should usually be stated at the end of the literature review**

In light of Guideline 6.6, it is logical to place research hypotheses, objectives, or questions at the end of a literature review.[2] Notice in Example 6.5.1 that the last topic (Topic 5) for the literature review is a statement of the research objectives.

> **Guideline 6.8 Research reports with similar findings or methodologies should usually be cited together**

This guideline is illustrated in Example 6.8.1. Notice that in the example, the information in the sentence is supported by two references.

Example 6.8.2 also illustrates this guideline. Notice that four references are cited in a single, cohesive paragraph dealing with one topic.

Example 6.8.1

The fit between a student and the institution, which is particular to the students' academic and personal preferences, needs, and interests is associated with higher student satisfaction and intent to persist (Bowman & Denson, 2014; Gilbreath, Kim, & Nichols, 2011).[3]

Example 6.8.2

It is well established that participation in student activities affects college undergraduates' level of alcohol consumption (Wechslet, Davenport, Dowdall, & Castillo, 1995; Turrisi, Mallet, & Mastroleo, 2006). More recently, it was suggested that it is the social capital cultivated through interactions with others that occur within the context of student activities that underlies these effects (Buettner & Debies-Carl, 2012; Theall et al., 2009).[4]

> **Guideline 6.9 The importance of a topic should be explicitly stated**

It can be a mistake to assume that readers already know the importance of a problem. Even if they are aware that a problem is of some importance, they may not be aware of its seriousness or all its implications.

Typically, the importance of the topic should be established near the beginning of a literature review. Be specific in giving reasons for the importance of the topic, as illustrated in Example 6.9.1, which is the beginning of the first paragraph in a literature review.

Example 6.9.1

The risk of sudden cardiac arrest (SCA) disproportionately impacts minorities and men, resulting in higher rates of neurological injury, disability, and mortality (Fender et al., 2014). Main risk factors of SCA are linked to external diseases that are prevalent in minority populations, including diabetes, COPD, bronchial asthma, and mental and behavioral disorders (e.g., drug use) (Fender et al., 2014; Graham, 2015; McNally et al., 2011; Uchmanowicz et al., 2015 ...).[5]

Note that nonspecific statements of importance are inappropriate. For instance, the statement in Example 6.9.2 was made in a proposal for a thesis in which a functional skills program in adult schools was to be evaluated. Notice that the statement fails to deal specifically with functional skills in adult education. In fact, the statement is so broad that it could refer to almost any curriculum and instruction topic in education.

Example 6.9.2

Nonspecific statement of importance (not recommended): Human resource is one of the greatest resources of this country, and education plays a major role in maintaining, nurturing, and protecting that resource. Thus, it is imperative that we find, evaluate, and utilize educational systems that yield the results necessary for the country's progress.

➤ **Guideline 6.10 Consider pointing out the number or percentage of individuals who are affected by the problem**

Showing that many individuals are affected by a problem helps to establish the importance of a research project. When possible, the specific numbers and percentages should be indicated—not just referred to in the form of nonspecific generalizations such as "A large percentage of high school students report that ..." or "An increasing number of individuals have ..."

The authors of Example 6.10.1 provide specific percentages.

Example 6.10.1

In 2016, Black students comprised merely 4%, and Hispanic students only 11%, of engineering bachelor's degrees earned (NCSES 2019).[6]

In a similar fashion, the authors of Example 6.10.2 established the importance of community-based agencies and HIV prevention, with the obvious implication that thousands of individuals are affected.

Example 6.10.2

In 2015, the CDC awarded $216 million to 90 community-based agencies to deliver HIV prevention programs to populations most vulnerable to HIV infection and transmission, including racial and ethnic groups, men who have sex with men, transgender individuals, and individuals who use injectable drugs (Centers for Disease Control and Prevention National Center for HIV/AIDS Viral Hepatitis STD and TB Prevention, 2015).[7]

Note that Examples 6.10.1 and 6.10.2 were drawn from the first paragraphs of literature reviews. It is common for writers to begin literature reviews by reporting the numbers and percentages of individuals affected by a problem.

➤ **Guideline 6.11 Discuss theories that have relevance
to the current research**

A *theory* is a cohesive set of principles that helps explain relationships among variables. Pointing out how the research relates to theories helps to establish the context for the research and its importance. Discussion of theories can be integrated
throughout the literature review. Typically, the major propositions of a theory and
their implications (i.e., what they predict) should be briefly described, as is demonstrated in Example 6.11.1.

Example 6.11.1

The project was guided by critical race theory (CRT) as it has been articu-
lated in the US (Ladson-Billings, 1998) and, subsequently, in the UK (Hylton,
2012; Gillborn et al., 2018a). CRT explores how systemic forms of racism
within education have failed to acknowledge epistemological scholarship
of Global South authors, Indigenous authors and Global North authors of
colour (Ladson-Billings and Tate, 1995; Solórzano and Yosso, 2002; Hylton,
2012; Delgado and Stefancic, 2017). CRT focuses on the experiential knowledge of ethnic minorities with respect to race and race relations (Solórzano
and Yosso, 2002).[8]

Note that being able to show that a research project is theory-based is an important way to justify conducting a study because theory-building is a foundation that
helps the scientific community understand the relationships among findings.

➤ **Guideline 6.12 Consider commenting on the relevance and
importance of the research being cited**

If a study is especially relevant or important, consider mentioning it, as is done in
Examples 6.12.1 and 6.12.2. This is most commonly seen in a thesis or dissertation,
and is often much more implicit in the literature review of a journal article.

Example 6.12.1

The most revealing experiment on this topic was conducted by Doe (2022),
who used a novel treatment to demonstrate that …

Example 6.12.2

Of most relevance to the current research, the National Synthesis Survey (Smith, 2021) revealed that …

➤ **Guideline 6.13 Point out trends in the literature**

In Example 6.13.1, the researchers point out a trend within the literature.

Example 6.13.1

Several prior studies have compared the teaching practices of novice special education teachers who have and have not received formal teacher prepara- tion (e.g., Nougaret et al., 2005; Sindelair et al., 2004), while others have probed the importance of special education teacher preparation specifically for classroom reading practices (e.g., Bishop et al., 2010).[9]

➤ **Guideline 6.14 Point out gaps in the literature**

In Example 6.14.1, the researcher points out gaps in the literature on extracurricular activities and child development.

Example 6.14.1

In sum, the foregoing literature has offered initial insights into the role of extracurricular activities (EA) in child development, but has mostly exam- ined EAs and family circumstances in isolation, thereby preventing a deeper understanding of child development in multiple, possibly mutually interacting contexts. The few existing studies that included both EA and family contexts primarily focused on school-aged children and youth (Vandell et al., 2015). The interplay between EAs and other developmental contexts on children's development during early childhood is poorly understood, a gap that would be addressed in the current study.[10]

In Example 6.14.2, the researchers point out a gap in research on Undocumented Student Resource Centers (USRC).

Example 6.14.2

Heeding Muñoz et al.'s (2018) charge for institutions to reexamine how inaction reinforces racist structures, this study addresses an important gap in the research literature by exploring how USRCs have been developed within community colleges.[11]

Pointing out gaps is especially important when the purpose of the current research is to fill one or more of the gaps.

➤ **Guideline 6.15 Be prepared to justify statements regarding gaps in the literature**

Students who are writing term project papers, theses, and dissertations should note that when they point out gaps in the literature, they may be asked by their professors to defend such assertions. Thus, it is a good idea to keep careful records of how the literature search was conducted (e.g., what online indices and databases were examined, including the dates) and which descriptors and search parameters (e.g., subject index terms) were used.

Online research has its pluses and its minuses. While the use of the Internet as a research tool (e.g., library databases) and research site (e.g., online surveying, studying online activities, online ethnography) has exploded in recent years, one must be cautious on relying too heavily on online sources of information. Students should be keenly aware of the differences between reliable and unreliable information and should never disregard knowledge not easily found online. There is such a thing as "good" versus "bad" data, and it is imperative that students use their critical thinking skills when interpreting the use of statistics in the real world.

Students should consider including a statement such as the one in Example 6.15.1 in their reports.

Example 6.15.1

A search of the ABC Index for the years 1995 through 2020 using the subject index terms "term a" and "term b" yielded only two studies of adolescents (i.e., Doe, 2009; Jones, 2021) and no studies of children.

➤ **Guideline 6.16 Point out how the current study differs from previous studies**

It is usually desirable to point out how the current study differs from previous ones. The differences may be in terms of the selection of variables, how the variables were conceptualized and measured, the composition of the sample, the method of analysis, and so on. Example 6.16.1 illustrates how this might be done.

Example 6.16.1

All the studies reported previously relied on self-reports by adolescents as the source of the data. In the current study, reports by the parents of adolescents were used.

➤ Guideline 6.17 Use direct quotations sparingly

This guideline is suggested for three reasons. First, direct quotations often do not convey their full meaning when quoted out of context. Second, quotations may disrupt the flow of the review because of the varying writing styles of the authors. Finally, quotations sometimes bog down readers in details that are not essential for the purpose of obtaining an overview of the literature. By paraphrasing instead of quoting, minor details can be easily omitted.

Direct quotations are appropriate when the writer of the review (1) wants to illustrate either the original author's skill at writing (or lack thereof), or (2) believes that the wording of a statement will have an emotional impact on the reader that would be lost in paraphrase. These purposes seldom arise in presenting literature in an empirical research report.

Direct quotations are also appropriate when citing carefully crafted definitions that have been included in previous research reports. Chapter 7 provides guidelines on writing definitions.

➤ Guideline 6.18 Report sparingly on the details of the literature being cited

Because the research being cited has usually been published, readers can obtain copies to learn the details.

Typically, reviews of literature in theses and dissertations contain more details on cited research than reviews in research reports published as journal articles. Even in theses and dissertations, however, writers should be selective in reporting details. For instance, it may be appropriate to describe an especially relevant and seminal study in more detail than others.

It is also important to "tell your own story" about the literature that has been reviewed. Published research should be used to support a student's ideas rather than talking about a topic through citing others. As such, it may not be appropriate to cite every sentence in a paragraph. This, of course, requires a careful balance to avoid plagiarism.

➤ Guideline 6.19 Consider using literature to provide the historical context for the present study

Following this guideline is especially desirable in theses and dissertations where students should demonstrate that they have a comprehensive knowledge of the literature on their topic. It is also appropriate in research reports published as journal articles when researchers wish to (1) acknowledge the original proponents' theories and principles that underlie their current studies, or (2) show that their research is a logical continuation of the historical chain of thought on a topic.

Examples 6.19.1 and 6.19.2 show how the history of a topic might be briefly traced.

Example 6.19.1

Research in recent years has shown that mindfulness-based interventions can enhance teachers' mental and physical health. However, the existing studies were predominantly conducted in Western, educated, industrialized, rich, and democratic (WEIRD) societies. As a randomized controlled trial in a non-WEIRD society, the present study examined the effectiveness and mechanisms of mindfulness training for Hong Kong teachers in difficult times.[12]

Example 6.19.2

Although its origins date back over 100 years (Chapman, 1994), bodybuilding did not move into mainstream culture until the 1960s (Schwarzenegger & Dobbins, 1998). Since then, it has seen a steady rise in popularity. The National Physique Committee (NPC; personal communication, May 17, 2008) estimates their bodybuilding membership to be at 20,000, with an annual increase of 1,000 new members. The International Federation of Body Building (IFBB) estimates that their annual membership also increases by 1,000 members annually (IFBB, personal communication, May 17th, 2008). With its popular movement into American culture, bodybuilding is no longer a fringe activity.[13]

> ### Guideline 6.20 Consider citing prior literature reviews

Before citing prior literature reviews, examine the literature cited in the reviews to determine if the reviewers have accurately characterized the literature.

When citing prior reviews, summarize their major conclusions, and then bring readers up to date by discussing the literature published since the prior reviews were published.

> ### Guideline 6.21 When using the "author-date method" for citing references, decide whether to emphasize authorship or content

Note that in the author-date method for citing references (also known as the Harvard method)[14] only the authors' last names and year of publication are given within the text (with full bibliographic references provided in the reference list at the end).

In the author-date method, names may be made part of the sentence, as in Example 6.21.1. In Example 6.21.1, the emphasis is on the authorship.

Example 6.21.1

Doe (2023) reported that a major source or dissatisfaction among teachers appears to be the low social status accorded their profession.

As an alternative, the names may be included parenthetically, as in Example 6.21.2. By using the parenthetical method, writers emphasize the content of the statement, not its authorship.

Example 6.21.2

A major source or dissatisfaction among teachers appears to be the low social status accorded their profession (Doe, 2023).

Because a literature review should be an essay that integrates and evaluates the content of previous research on a topic, presenting the researcher's name in parentheses, as in Example 6.21.2, is usually preferable because it deemphasizes the authorship.

Of course, sometimes authorship is important and should be emphasized—for instance, when comparing the thoughts of two leading theorists.

➤ **Guideline 6.22 Avoid referring to the credentials and affiliations of the researchers**

In an appeal to authority, writers in the popular press often refer to a researcher's credentials (e.g., being a professor) and affiliations (e.g., Harvard University) when summarizing research. Thus, in a newspaper article on recently released research, it would not be uncommon to see a statement such as "Professor Doe of Harvard University's School of Public Health reported in an article published in the *Journal of Studies* that …" Such a statement in a formal academic report of empirical research should almost never be used because scholars' confidence in the results of a research study should rest on the strength of the evidence presented (in light of the care with which empirical methods were used in the research)—not on the credentials or affiliations of the researchers.

➤ **Guideline 6.23 Terminology in a literature review should reflect the tentative nature of empirical data**

Empirical research is inherently subject to error. Despite their best efforts, researchers conduct research with limitations. For instance, samples are often less than ideal, and measures are almost always less than perfectly valid and reliable. As a result, empirical data offer only degrees of evidence. Of course, some evidence is stronger than other evidence, so care should be used in how the evidence is described. As a result, the word *proof* or any of its derivatives (e.g., *proved*) should never be used to describe the results of an empirical study.

For studies that are reasonably strong (e.g., employing adequate samples and reasonable measures), statements such as those in Example 6.23.1 may be used (italics added for emphasis). Note that they are relatively neutral regarding the strength of the evidence.

Example 6.23.1

A recent study *indicates* that …
Two experiments *yielded evidence* that …
Doe (2023) *reported* that …

For studies that are very strong (e.g., employing excellent samples and highly valid and reliable measures), statements such as those in Example 6.23.2 may be used (italics added for emphasis). Note that they indicate that the evidence is strong.

Example 6.23.2

The results of a major national survey *strongly indicate* that …
Taken together, the experiments described above *provide strong evidence* that …
The result of Doe's (2022) seminal research *strongly suggests* that …

For studies that are very weak (e.g., clearly biased samples and measures of highly questionable validity and reliability), statements such as those in Example 6.23.3 may be used (italics added for emphasis). Note that they indicate that the evidence is weak.

Example 6.23.3

In a *preliminary pilot study*, Doe (2022) found that …
In *light of its methodological weaknesses*, the results of this study should be viewed …

While all of the experiments cited above suggest that X is more effective than Y, the failure to use random assignment *seriously limits confidence* in the results.

> ### Guideline 6.24 Avoid using long strings of reference citations for a single finding or theory

Some findings or theories have been very widely reported in the literature. Suppose, for instance, that there are 32 journal articles that reported data that support the XYZ theory. It would be distracting as well as unproductive to make a simple statement to this effect followed by 32 reference citations in parentheses. One solution is to simply use *e.g.* (which stands for "for example") and cite only a few, as illustrated in Example 6.24.1.

Example 6.24.1

More than 30 experiments reported in journal articles have lent support to the XYZ theory (e.g., Doe, 2002; Jones, 2016; Lopez, 2020).

Another solution is to indicate the time span over which the support has been reported while citing only some of the early and some of the more recent experiments, as in Example 6.24.2.

Example 6.24.2

More than 30 experiments reported in journal articles have lent support to the XYZ theory, starting with studies conducted more than 50 years ago (e.g., Barnes, 1960; Black, 1952) and continuing to the present (Jones, 2019; Smith & Smith, 2022).

Still another solution is to cite only those that are strongest in terms of research methodology, as in Example 6.24.3.

Example 6.24.3

More than 30 experiments reported in journal articles have lent support to the XYZ theory. Among these, three used true experimental designs with random assignment to treatment groups (Banner & Brown, 2019; Cive, 2020; Tanner, 2015).

Yet another solution is to distinguish among the reports based on the strength of their support, as in Example 6.24.4.

Example 6.24.4

More than 30 experiments reported in journal articles have lent support to the XYZ theory. While the support is weak in about half the studies (e.g., Ariztia, 2009; Green, 2019), stronger support has been reported in the others (e.g., Schumacher, 2011; White, 2021).

In a thesis or dissertation, students may be expected to cite all relevant references to demonstrate that a comprehensive literature search has been conducted. Even in this circumstance, long strings of citations can be avoided by referring to the references in smaller groups. For instance, the methodologically stronger ones can be cited in one group while weaker ones can be cited in another. Other examples are (1) citing studies that use one approach (e.g., experiments) in a separate group from those that use a different approach (e.g., surveys), (2) separating older studies from newer studies, and (3) calling special attention to a study that represents a turning point in understanding an issue.

➤ **Guideline 6.25 Use of the first person is acceptable if used sparingly.**

Use of the first person is especially appropriate when referring to the author's personal observations, experiences, and beliefs, as is the case in Example 6.25.1. The use of "I" in this example is less stilted than using the term *the author* to refer to the writer.

Example 6.25.1

I began to speculate on the origins of this problem during my three years as a teacher assistant within the New York City public school system.

However, frequent use of the first person throughout the introduction and elsewhere in a research report can be distracting. It is especially inappropriate when referring to matters that are not personal, such as the lack of experimental studies mentioned in Example 6.25.2.

Example 6.25.2

When I realized that all the previous research on this topic was nonexperimental, I decided that it would be especially important for me to conduct an experimental study for the current investigation.

Improved Version of Example 6.25.2

Because all the previous research on this topic was nonexperimental, it seemed especially important to conduct an experimental study for the current investigation.

➤ **Guideline 6.26 In long literature reviews, start with a paragraph that describes its organization and use subheadings**

The numbered topics in the example near the beginning of this chapter (Example 6.5.1: "Importance of question-asking by children" and "Introduction to two basic types of questions") could be used as subheadings within the literature review.

In theses and dissertations, where introductions and literature reviews each are fairly long chapters, the use of subheadings is especially desirable. Begin each chapter with an overview of what is covered in it and begin each subsection with such an overview. This is illustrated in Example 6.26.1, in which the first paragraph provides an overview of the chapter, and the second paragraph provides an overview of the first subsection. The third paragraph then begins a discussion of the topic covered by the first subsection with citations to the literature (i.e., "Two major studies ...").

It may be appropriate to provide a hypothesis statement at the end of a given rationale. In other words, the literature review may be peppered with hypotheses for study throughout, as it moves from one subheading/topic to another.

Example 6.26.1

Chapter 2
Literature Review

This chapter describes literature relevant to the research purposes of this thesis. It is organized into four sections: (1) the importance of question-asking by children, (2) an introduction to two basic types of questions, (3) the relationship between parents' and children's verbal behavior, and (4) the relationship between culture and verbal behavior. At the end of each section, the relevance of the literature to the research reported in this thesis is discussed.

Importance of Question-Asking by Children

Most of the literature on the importance of question-asking deals with the behavior of students in school settings during learning activities. This literature is reviewed first in order to establish the importance of question-asking as a tool in the learning/teaching process. Then, the more limited literature on the importance of question-asking by children as a functional skill in the home and other non-school settings is reviewed. Throughout, there is an emphasis on the principles of learning theories as well as theories of social interaction that underlie the literature.

Two major studies examined the relationship between students' question-asking behavior and …

➤ **Guideline 6.27 Consider ending long and complex literature reviews with a brief summary**

This guideline is illustrated in Example 6.27.1.

Example 6.27.1

In summary, dialectical thinking (e.g., avoiding "all or nothing" thinking), optimism, mindfulness, and cognitive reappraisal are all possible strategies to mitigate the negative impact of social media on mental health during the COVID-19 pandemic.[15]

Concluding Comments

If you lack confidence in your ability to write introductions and literature reviews, follow these suggestions:

1. Write a topic outline, as illustrated in Example 6.5.1, and take it with you when you consult with your instructor or committee. The outline will help them understand what you are trying to accomplish and make it easier for them to offer guidance.
2. Read numerous reviews of literature, paying attention to how they are organized and how the authors make transitions from one topic to another.
3. After writing a first draft, have it reviewed by friends and colleagues—even if they are not experts on the topic of the review. Ask them to point out elements that are not clear. Note that effective introductions and literature reviews are usually comprehensible to any intelligent layperson.
4. Be prepared to revise and rewrite. Because effective writing is achieved through revising and rewriting, expect your instructor, committee, or journal editor to request revisions.

Exercises for Chapter 6

Please note that because the application of many of the guidelines in this chapter involves a certain amount of subjectivity, there may be differences of opinions on the best answers to some of the following questions.

Part A

1. "In theses and dissertations, literature reviews are selective, including references only to the most relevant literature." According to this chapter, is this statement true or false?

2. What is wrong with preparing a list of annotations and using it as a literature review (e.g., what does a list of annotations fail to do)?

3. To implement Guideline 6.5, what should be done first?

4. "It is logical to place research hypotheses, objectives, or questions at the beginning of a literature review." According to this chapter, is this statement true or false?

5. Critique the following paragraph, which was submitted by a student to indicate the importance of their research topic (the prevalence of depression among inner-city adolescents).

In the new millennium, the public is increasingly aware of the importance of the psychological well-being of all citizens. Because of this recognition by the public, it is important to conduct more studies that shed light on the prevalence of well-being, starting with the psychological well-being of adolescents, who will soon be adults.

6. Showing that many individuals are affected by a problem helps to establish what?

7. Is it important to be able to show that a research project is theory-based?

8. When is pointing out gaps in the literature especially important?

9. How can a student prepare to justify statements regarding gaps in the literature?

10. A student wrote a literature review with a large number of quotations from the literature in the belief that the quotations would substantiate the points being made. According to this chapter, is this appropriate? Explain.

11. Should citations to older literature be avoided?

12. Is it ever appropriate to cite prior literature reviews?

13. Does the following statement cited using the author-date method emphasize "authorship" or "content"? Explain.

The superiority of the Alpha method for teaching secondary-level science has recently been demonstrated in an experiment with randomized experimental and control groups (Doe, 2021).

14. Critique the following statement from a literature review.

Dr. Richard Doe (2023), Professor of Education at Stanford University, reported on the effects of variable schedules of reinforcement on the mathematics achievement of …

15. Critique the following statement from a literature review.

These two experiments unequivocally prove that the XYZ method is superior …

16. Is the use of the first person ever acceptable?

Part B

17. Examine the literature reviews of three recently published research reports (either journal articles, theses, or dissertations) on a topic of interest to you and answer the following questions.

A. In how many instances does the author explicitly state why the research topic is important and cite specific numbers or percentages to support the statement? Take note of any examples you find.

B. In how many instances does the author cite references to relevant theories? If any, what are the names of the theories? Are the discussions of the theories brief or in-depth?

C. Overall, do the authors use terminology that reflects the tentative nature of empirical data? (See Guideline 6.23.)

D. In how many cases are direct quotations from the literature included?

Part C

Write a brief topic outline for a literature review for a research project of interest to you. Have it reviewed by two friends or colleagues and revise it in light of their comments.

Notes

1. Almond, Parson, & Resor (2021, pp. 1600–1601).
2. As noted in Guideline 6.1, the research hypotheses, objectives, or questions are usually stated at the end of Chapter 1 (the Introduction) and may be restated at the end of Chapter 2 (the Literature Review) in theses and dissertations; see Guideline 6.2.
3. Holland (2020, p. 379).
4. Crawford & Novak (2020, p. 9).
5. Lee, Muller, & McDermott (2021, p. 5).
6. Main, Johnson, & Wang (2021, p. 449).
7. Pinto, Kay, Choi, & Wall (2020, pp. 970–971).
8. Adewumi et al. (2022, p. 3).
9. Theobald, Goldhaber, Holden, & Stein (2022, p. 382).
10. Ren et al. (2021, p. 1032).
11. Freeman-Wong, Mazumder, & Cisneros (2022, p. 437).
12. Tsang et al. (2021, p. 2820).
13. Parish, Baghurst, & Turner (2010, p. 152).
14. This method has been popularized by the *Publication Manual of the American Psychological Association* and is in widespread use throughout the social and behavioral sciences.
15. Haddad et al. (2021, p. 7).

Chapter 7

Writing Definitions

Two types of definitions are usually found in empirical research reports. A *conceptual definition*, which resembles dictionary definitions, indicates the general meaning of a concept. These are usually presented in the introduction and/or literature review. *Operational definitions*, which define traits in concrete, step-by-step physical terms, are usually presented in the section on methods. (See Example 1.7.1 in Chapter 1 to review the structure of a basic research report.)

This chapter presents guidelines on what to define and how to write both conceptual and operational definitions.

> ➤ **Guideline 7.1 All variables in a research hypothesis, objective, or question should be defined**

Example 7.1.1 is a hypothesis. "Online news reading habits" and "cultural literacy" need to be defined in the research report.

Example 7.1.1

It is hypothesized that there is a direct relationship between online news reading habits and cultural literacy.

At the conceptual level, "online news reading habits" might be generally defined in terms of "regularity of referring to online news websites for information and entertainment."

At the operational (i.e., physical) level, the definition might refer to the daily average number of minutes spent reading online news sites, the typical number of articles read, whether individuals subscribe to specific sites (e.g., *The New York Times*), how often individuals consult news websites/apps, and so on.

Obviously, how online news reading habits are defined at the operational level could have an important influence on the results of the study for the hypothesis in Example 7.1.1. For instance, using "number of minutes spent reading online news" as the operational definition might yield different data than using "how often individuals consult news websites/apps."

➤ Guideline 7.2 The defining attributes of a population (also called *control variables*) should be defined

In the hypothesis in Example 7.2.1, "adult education learners" is a defining attribute that should be specifically defined.

Example 7.2.1

There is a direct relationship between newspaper reading habits and cultural literacy among adult education learners.

In Example 7.2.2, the definition of "adult education learners" is not as specific as it could be. The improved version contains more details than the original version. These details help readers understand the characteristics of the population.

Example 7.2.2

"Adult education learners" are adults enrolled in formal education programs.

Improved Version of Example 7.2.2

"Adult education learners" are individuals over 18 years of age who are enrolled in one or more classes in adult schools operated by the Los Angeles Unified School District.

➤ Guideline 7.3 Key concepts in theories on which the research is based should be defined

The "stress–coping theory" is mentioned in Example 7.3.1. (Note that the researchers provide a reference where more information on the theory can be found.)

Example 7.3.1

Stress-coping theory indicates that maladaptive coping strategies involve individuals' behavioral attempts to decrease their level of discomfort when they are maintaining negative emotional states (Liu et al, 2021; Zhang, Ding, & Ma, 2022).[1]

The researchers who wrote Example 7.3.1 devote a large paragraph to a description of the tenets of this theory. In addition, they present the definition of coping theory more generally. They define coping theory as it relates to social media use in Example 7.3.2.

Example 7.3.2

In social media use and consumer behavioral studies, coping theory has been explained as the way individuals adapt to and handle social media overload.[2]

> **Guideline 7.4 A conceptual definition should be sufficiently specific to differentiate it from related concepts**

Even though a conceptual definition indicates only the general meaning of a concept, the conceptual definition should be sufficiently specific to differentiate it from related concepts. Consider Example 7.4.1, which provides context on the specific types of "resources" included in the authors' definition.

Example 7.4.1

Resources are defined broadly to include personal characteristics (e.g., demographic factors, role beliefs, personality traits), interpersonal relationships (e.g., the coparenting relationship and social support networks), and contextual characteristics (e.g., family structure, societal values, and social class) associated with how fathers parent their children.[3]

> **Guideline 7.5 Consider quoting published conceptual definitions**

As indicated by Guideline 6.17 in the previous chapter, direct quotations from literature should be used sparingly. Quoting definitions, however, is not only acceptable, it can be superior to creating new definitions if the quoted definitions have been carefully thought out and reviewed by other experts. This is often the case in journal articles that have been critiqued by an editorial board.

The author of Example 7.5.1 quotes a definition of "heteronormativity."

Example 7.5.1

Heteronormativity refers to social and cultural practices that "derive from and reinforce a set of taken-for-granted presumptions relating to sex and gender" (Kitzinger, 2005).[4]

➤ **Guideline 7.6 Consider providing examples to amplify conceptual definitions**

Providing one or more examples can often make the meaning of a definition clear. In Example 7.4.1, the researchers provide parenthetical examples of included concepts.

➤ **Guideline 7.7 Operational definitions usually should be provided in the Method section of a report**

An operational definition is one that is stated in terms of physical steps. While conceptual definitions are often presented in the introduction/literature review, operational definitions are usually presented in the section on methods.[5] (See Example 1.7.1 in Chapter 1 to review the structure of a basic research report.)

It is especially important to provide operational definitions within the Measures subsection of the section on methods in order to operationalize measurement procedures. Compare Example 7.7.1 with its improved version. The improved version has been operationalized by referring to the physical steps used to measure the variable of "desire for thinness."

Example 7.7.1

Desire for thinness was determined based on the girls' ratings of themselves in relation to silhouette drawings of very thin to very fat girls.

Improved Version of Example 7.7.1

Desire for thinness was measured with the girls' version of the Children's Figure Rating Scale (Tiggemann & Wilson-Barrett, 1998). This scale presents on an A3-sized bright-colored piece of cardboard with nine young female silhouette drawings, ranging from very thin to very fat. Girls were asked, "Which girl

---

do you think you look like?" (current figure), followed by "Which girl would you most like to look like?" (ideal figure). Girls responded by simply pointing to their choices. Desire for thinness was calculated as current minus ideal figure rating. Good test retest reliability has been found for such figure rating scales with children as young as 6 to 7 years of age (Collins, 1991).[6]

In reports on experiments, the steps taken to treat the experimental groups should be operationalized in the section on methods. Compare Example 7.7.2 (which is not very operational) with its improved version, which describes physical conditions and steps.

Example 7.7.2

The stress-producing condition for the experimental group was a mild verbal threat given by the experimenter.

Improved Version of Example 7.7.2

In order to produce the stress-producing condition for the experimental group, a male experimenter dressed in a white doctor's jacket seated the participants. He introduced himself as a physician with a specialty in internal medicine and stated that for the purposes of the experiment, "You will receive a mild electric shock while we measure your blood pressure."

➤ Guideline 7.8 Consider providing operational definitions for each conceptual definition

For each conceptual definition, consider providing an operational definition in the section on methods. A conceptual definition of a "bias crime" and a corresponding operational definition are provided in Example 7.8.1.

Example 7.8.1

Conceptual definition in the Introduction

In the United States, states utilize a variety of definitions of bias crimes, but the federal government defines them as "criminal offense against a person or property motivated in whole or in part by an offender's bias against a race, religion, disability, sexual orientation, ethnicity, gender, or gender identity" (Federal Bureau of Investigation, 2016).[7]

> *Corresponding operational definition in the Method section*
>
> Bias crimes have many distinguishing features, such as being committed by groups of perpetrators (Craig, 2002) who are strangers to the victim/s (Messner, McHugh, & Felson, 2004), and that occur in open or public spaces (Messner et al., 2004) in larger percentages than non-bias crimes. Bias crimes are also more likely to be crimes against persons as opposed to crimes against property (FBI, 2015), and to cause more injury or harm to victims (Levin, 1992; Messner et al., 2004) than non-bias crimes.[8]

In Example 7.8.1, the operational definition is sufficiently specific that it rules out alternative methods of defining the variable.

> ## ➤ Guideline 7.9 If a published measure was used, the variable measured by it may be operationally defined by citing reference(s)

A published measure,[9] such as an achievement test, almost always comes with specific, step-by-step physical directions for its use. By citing the test with a reference to the author and publisher of the test, a researcher can provide an operational definition. Example 7.9.1 provides such a definition.

> ## Example 7.9.1
>
> Beginning mathematics skill was defined as the composite score on Form S of the Primary Level 2 multiple-choice/open-ended Mathematics Test of the Stanford Achievement Test Series, Tenth Edition (Harcourt Brace, 2022).

To further operationalize the definition in Example 7.9.1, the author could provide an overview of the physical properties of the test (e.g., content of the items, numbers of multiple-choice and open-ended items, time limits), and the statistical properties of the test, especially reliability and validity.

> ## ➤ Guideline 7.10 If an unpublished measure was used, consider reproducing sample questions or the entire measure

For specialized research purposes, researchers often construct their own measures (e.g., tests, scales, and checklists). If such a measure is very short, a copy may be included in the research report. Longer measures should be included in appendices in term projects, theses, and dissertations, but usually are not included in research reports published in journal articles. Authors of journal articles should be prepared to supply copies of longer, unpublished measures to readers who request them.

Examples 7.10.1 and 7.10.2 illustrate this guideline.

Example 7.10.1

Qualtrics will then direct consenting participants to the job ad for a Human Resources Manager position (see S2 Appendix). The job ad page will also include a set of questions about the position to help draw the participant's attention to this information. These questions assess the participant's recall about the position, its responsibilities and roles, and both required and preferred qualifications (see S2 Appendix). Participants will not be able to advance past this stage until five minutes have elapsed and they have answered each of these questions.[10]

Example 7.10.2

The Visual Scanning Test is a new neuropsychological instrument based on perceptual tasks that investigate extrapersonal space. Due to the lack of neuropsychological instruments to assess visual searching in far space, the VST may be used to detect visual searching alterations and the availability of normative data allows its utilization in clinical practice.[11]

➤ **Guideline 7.11 Operational definitions should be specific enough so that another researcher can replicate the study**

A *replication* is an attempt to reproduce the results of a previous study by using the same research methods. Replicability is the major criterion for judging the reliability and validity of the results of empirical research.

Even definitions that appear to be highly operational at first glance may be inadequate when a researcher attempts to replicate a study. The definition in Example 7.11.1 illustrates this point. When a researcher prepares to replicate a study involving "visual acuity," questions about the physical process arise: How large were the letters? What font was used? What size/type of screen was used? and so on. Answers to these questions could easily affect individuals' ability to recognize letters of the alphabet flashed on a screen.

Example 7.11.1

Visual acuity was defined as the ability to name the letters of the alphabet when flashed on a screen in a random order for a period of two seconds for each letter.

This guideline is often not followed to the letter. In practice, a writer should consider how operational a definition needs to be to permit a reasonably close replication. For making fine discriminations among very similar shapes, answers to the questions posed about Example 7.11.1 may be crucial to a successful replication.

➤ Guideline 7.12 Even a highly operational definition may not be a useful definition

An operational definition that is too narrow or is too different from how most other individuals define a variable may be inadequate. Example 7.12.1 illustrates this point. It provides a fairly operational definition of self-concept, but the definition is much narrower than that used by most psychologists and teachers.

Example 7.12.1

Self-concept was defined as the number of times each child smiled during the first 15 minutes of homeroom for five consecutive days. A smile was defined as a noticeable upward turn where the lips meet—based on agreement by three independent observers. Each observer was a graduate student in clinical psychology. Counts of smiles were made from video recordings, which permitted the observers to re-examine facial expressions that were questionable.

Concluding Comments

Writing satisfactory operational definitions is sometimes more difficult than it might appear at first. When writing them, assume that you are telling someone exactly how to conduct your study. Then have the first draft of the definitions reviewed by colleagues and ask them if they could perform the same study in the same way without requesting additional information.

As a general rule, it is best to provide lengthy, detailed operational definitions so that readers can be confident that they understand them.

Exercises for Chapter 7

Part A

For each of the following definitions, describe what additional types of information, if any, are needed to make it more operational.

1. Language skill was defined as scores on a scale from 1 to 10 on an essay test that required students to write three essays in a 50-minute class period.

2. Depression was defined as the raw score on the Second Edition of Doe's Depression Inventory for Adults (Doe, 2023).

3. Computer phobia was defined as clear signs of anxiety when being seated in front of a computer.

4. Hispanic students were defined as those students whose surnames appeared on a master list of Latinx surnames developed by the author in consultation with a linguist. This list may be obtained by emailing the author at jdoe@university.edu.

5. Potential high school dropouts were defined as those who have a poor attitude toward school.

6. Discrimination was defined as acts against individuals that limit their opportunities solely because of preconceived biases against the groups to which the individuals belong.

Part B

For each of the following variables, write a highly operational definition. Because you may not have studied some of these variables, do not concern yourself with whether your definitions are highly useful. (See Guideline 7.12.) Instead, make them sufficiently operational so that they would make a study of them replicable. (See Guideline 7.11.)

7. Political involvement

8. Math anxiety

9. Ability to form friendships

10. Desire to achieve in school

Part C

Name a variable you might want to study. Write a conceptual definition and a highly operational definition of it. (For this activity, do not cite a published test or scale in order to define the variable you have selected.) Have the first draft of your definitions reviewed by colleagues, and then revise them.

Part D

Examine three research articles in journals, theses, or dissertations. Note how the variables are defined. Copy the definition you think is most operational.

Notes

1 Chung, Chen, & Meng (2023, p. 2).
2 Ibid.
3 Schoppe-Sullivan, Shafer, Olofson, & Kamp Dush (2021, p. 539).
4 Zsila, Orosz, McCutcheon, & Demetrovics (2021, p. 1336).
5 Another arrangement is to provide both conceptual and operational definitions in the section on methods.
6 Dohnt & Tiggemann (2006, p. 930).
7 Stotzer, Godinet, & Davidson (2020, p. 35).
8 Ibid. (p. 36).
9 In research, the term *instruments* is synonymous with the term *measures*.
10 Beasley & Xiao (2023, p. 8).
11 Borsotti et al. (2020, p. 1149).

Chapter 8

Writing Assumptions, Limitations, and Delimitations

An *assumption* is a condition that is believed to be true even though the direct evidence of its truth is either absent or very limited. A *limitation* is a weakness or handicap that potentially limits the validity of the results, while a *delimitation* is a boundary to which a study was deliberately confined.

Authors of research reports published in journal articles often integrate statements of assumptions, limitations, and delimitations in various sections of their articles, including the Introduction, Method section, and very frequently in the Discussion section at the end of the report. These authors usually are very selective in deciding which ones to state, naming only the major ones. Students who are writing term projects, theses, and dissertations are often expected to discuss these issues in some detail in order to show that they understand the concepts. In theses and dissertations, the assumptions, limitations, and delimitations are sometimes described in separate subsections of one of the chapters—often, the first chapter or the last chapter.

> **Guideline 8.1 When stating an assumption, consider providing the reason(s) why it was necessary to make the assumption**

In Example 8.1.1, this guideline has not been followed because, while it states what was assumed, it does not state why the assumption was necessary. Because no measure of human behavior is perfectly valid, Example 8.1.1 adds little to the research report. In the first sentence of the improved version, the authors describe the circumstances that led to the use of a scale that may have limited validity.

DOI: 10.4324/9781003230410-9   81

> ### Example 8.1.1
>
> It was assumed that the cheerfulness scale was valid.
>
> ***Improved Version of Example 8.1.1***
>
> Because we did not have the resources to make direct observations and ratings of cheerfulness over time in a variety of settings, we constructed a self-report measure of cheerfulness. It was necessary to assume that the participants were honest in self-reporting their typical levels of cheerfulness. To encourage honest responses, the cheerfulness scale was administered anonymously, and the participants were encouraged to be open and honest by the research assistant who administered the survey.

➤ Guideline 8.2 If there is a reason for believing that an assumption is true, state the reason

The last sentence in the improved version of Example 8.1.1 suggests a basis for believing that the assumption is true. Likewise, the last sentence in Example 8.2.1 provides the basis for such a belief.

> ### Example 8.2.1
>
> Because the investigator could not be present in all the classrooms while the experimental method was being used, it was necessary to assume that the teachers consistently and conscientiously used the experimental method of instruction. This assumption seems tenable because the teachers were given intensive training in the method, as described in the Method section of this report, and they reported enthusiasm for the method, as described in the Results section.

➤ Guideline 8.3 If an assumption is highly questionable, consider casting it as a limitation

Example 8.3.1 refers to a common flaw in research: use of a small sample. Unless a researcher has some empirical basis for believing that those in the small sample are representative of the larger population, it would be better to describe this problem as a limitation, as is done in the improved version. Note that researchers should not use assumptions to "wish away" fundamental flaws.

Example 8.3.1

It is assumed that the results we obtained with our small sample are generalizable to the larger population.

Improved Version of Example 8.3.1

The preservice teachers participating in this study were all from one faculty of education, albeit from different campuses and so the findings may not generalize to preservice teachers in other faculties of education across Canada.[1]

➤ **Guideline 8.4 Distinguish between limitations and delimitations**

As indicated at the beginning of this chapter, a *limitation* is a weakness or handicap that potentially limits the validity of the results, while a *delimitation* is a boundary to which a study was deliberately confined.

To understand the difference between a limitation and a delimitation, consider a researcher who wants to study artistic creativity in general but uses only a measure of creative drawing. This would be a limitation because it is a weakness in the execution of the study (i.e., measuring only creative drawing when the purpose is to study artistic creativity in general). In contrast, if the researcher's purpose is only to study creative drawing and the researcher deliberately chooses a measure of creative drawing, the findings would be delimited to this type of creativity, which is not a flaw in light of the researcher's purpose.

➤ **Guideline 8.5 Discuss limitations and delimitations separately**

Because they are separate issues, discuss the limitations (methodological weaknesses or flaws) in separate paragraphs or sections from delimitations (boundaries to which the study was deliberately limited).

➤ **Guideline 8.6 Consider elaborating on the nature of a limitation**

Instead of merely stating that the type of teacher studied was a limitation of their study, the authors of Example 8.6.1 elaborate in their discussion of this limitation.

Example 8.6.1

The preservice teachers enrolled in this study may also differ from in-service teachers who would be exposed to the same online intervention. These potential differences may be of such a nature as to limit extrapolation of these

---

results to in-service teachers. However, previous research studies have shown similar outcomes for preservice and in-service teachers exposed to the same face-to-face intervention, and it would not be unreasonable to suggest that similar results could be expected with online exposure as well. Replication of this study amongst in-service teachers should be undertaken to test this consideration.[2]

➤ Guideline 8.7 Consider speculating on the possible effects of a limitation on the results of a study

The authors of Example 8.7.1 speculate that their results may underestimate student performance because the data were collected via an optional quiz.[3]

Example 8.7.1

In addition, due to the fact that participation was optional, the stakes were not as high as they would have been for material required for a course and a quiz that counted toward the course grade. The quiz was similar to pre-lecture quizzes given in these courses, which are shorter and, perhaps, easier than a typical exam; therefore, these results may not generalize to more difficult material.[4]

➤ Guideline 8.8 If a study has serious limitations, consider labeling it a pilot study

A *pilot study* is an exploratory study that is used to try out and refine instruments, see if participants will be cooperative, check for preliminary support for a hypothesis, and so on. When this guideline is followed, it is sometimes done in the title, with a subtitle such as "A Pilot Study."

Researchers who conduct pilot studies often mention this status in several places in their research reports. For instance, the researchers who conducted the study cited in Example 8.8.1 mentioned that they conducted a pilot study in the title, in the Abstract, and in the Discussion section of their report.

Example 8.8.1

"Pilot study" mentioned in the title: A Pilot Study Assessing Effectiveness of a Written Shame Induction Protocol With and Without a Social Evaluative Threat Manipulation.

"Pilot study" mentioned in the Abstract: This pilot study was the first to evaluate the impact of a social evaluative threat (SET) manipulation on the shame induction effectiveness of a written shame protocol.

"Pilot study" mentioned in the Discussion section: The purpose of this pilot study was to investigate the impact of adding SET on the shame induction effectiveness of a novel, written shame protocol.[5]

➤ Guideline 8.9 Consider pointing out strengths as well as limitations

While it is important to warn readers of the limitations of a study, it is equally important to point out special strengths that make the study noteworthy. While this may be done in various sections of a report, it is often appropriate to point out strengths immediately before or after describing limitations, which are most often described in the Discussion section. (See Example 1.7.1 in Chapter 1 to review the structure of basic research reports.)

In Example 8.9.1, the authors outline their study's strengths.

Example 8.9.1

Our study also has several strengths. We had laboratory-quality measurements brought to an everyday school environment. All students had an equal opportunity to participate during the day, and participation was not limited or influenced by, for example, parental motivation to visit a clinic. As we had the unique opportunity to record physiological reactivity in a familiar environment, we gained information beyond laboratory conditions on stressful situations that children and adolescents may experience during their school day. This was also the first study in the field of psychophysiological measurement to include a follow-up past the immediate postintervention assessments.[6]

Exercises for Chapter 8

Part A

1. Suppose a researcher emailed a survey to each member of a population but only 8% completed and returned the survey. Further, suppose the researcher has no information on how the nonrespondents differ from the respondents. In your opinion, should the researcher assume that the sample is sound or should the researcher state that the nonresponse rate is a limitation? Explain.

2. Suppose a researcher's purpose was to examine adolescent girls' knowledge of nutrition. If the researcher included only adolescent girls as participants in the study (e.g., excluding adolescent boys), should the inclusion of only adolescent girls be considered a "limitation" or a "delimitation"?

3. Suppose a researcher used a standardized test that had been validated for the type of population being studied. Furthermore, suppose the test had high validity but, as with all tests, was somewhat less than perfectly valid. In your opinion, should the researcher describe this circumstance as a limitation? Would it be reasonable for the researcher to assume that the test is valid? Why?

Part B

4. Consider a research project that you plan to undertake. If you know of an assumption you would probably need to make, write a statement describing it.

5. Consider a research project you plan to undertake. If you know of a limitation (e.g., methodological flaw) that you would probably have if you conducted the study, write a statement describing it. For the same study, describe a delimitation to which your study probably would be confined.

Part C

6. Examine two research reports published in journals, theses, or dissertations that contain explicit statements of assumptions and/or limitations. Copy their relevant portions.

7. How many of the individual assumptions/limitations that you examined for Question 6 involved sampling? How many involved the instruments? How many involved other issues? Name them.

Notes

1 Wei, Carr, Alaffe, & Kutcher (2020, p. 112).
2 Ibid.
3 Of course, interviews have some advantages over questionnaires, such as providing more flexibility and allowing researchers to probe for additional information.
4 Austin, Fogler, & Daniel (2022, p. 372).
5 McGarity-Shipley, Jadidi, & Pyke (2022, pp. 257–267).
6 Lassander et al. (2022, pp. 314–315).

Chapter 9

Writing Method Sections

The Method section follows the literature review. (See Example 1.7.1 in Chapter 1 to review the structure of a basic research report.) The section on methods describes the steps taken to investigate the research question(s) as well as the reasons why the specific procedures or techniques were chosen to better understand the research topic. This section should answer the following two questions: (1) how was the information collected or generated? (2) how was it analyzed?

➢ Guideline 9.1 Provide a brief overview of the method used

It is important to begin the Method section by providing a brief overview of the method used (e.g., experiment, survey, ethnography, etc.).

Example 9.1.1

To gain insight into our students' perception of online learning, we formed an anonymous online survey which was filled out on a voluntary basis.[1]

➢ Guideline 9.2 Describe the sample

Immediately under the main heading of "Method" (centered in bold) should appear the subheading "Sample" or "Participants" (flush left in bold). As indicated in the next guideline, the term *Subjects* may be substituted for *Participants* under certain circumstances.

A portion of Example 1.4.1 in Chapter 1 is reproduced here as Example 9.2.1 to show the placement of the material on participants (see the arrow in the example).

 DOI: 10.4324/9781003230410-10

> **Example 9.2.1**
>
> Title in Upper- and Lowercase Letters
Abstract (a main heading; centered in bold)
> A literature review that introduces the research problem (with no heading)
> **Method** (a main heading; centered in bold)
> **Participants** (a subheading; flush left in bold)
> **Measures** (a subheading; flush left in bold)

➤ **Guideline 9.3 If applicable, decide whether to use the term**
   ***participants* or *subjects* to refer to the individuals**
   studied

Subjects is the traditional term used to refer to individuals studied in empirical research. Increasingly, researchers are using the term *participants* to refer to these individuals.[2] *Sample* is a better heading for studies involving units of observation different from the individual level (e.g., cities, dorms, etc.) or non-human samples (e.g., social media posts, archival data, etc.).

When individuals freely consent to participate in a study, it is logical to call them participants instead of subjects. However, sometimes researchers conduct research without obtaining consent. A clear example is a study of animal behavior, in which case it makes sense to refer to the animals as *subjects* in a report of the research.

Some studies of humans also do not involve consent to participate. For instance, if a researcher is conducting an observational study of the behavior of adolescents on Twitter, the researcher does not need consent to observe these public behaviors. In a report of such a study, the term *subjects* is more appropriate than the term *participants* because the adolescents are not knowingly participating and, of course, have not consented to participate.

➤ **Guideline 9.4 Describe the informed consent procedures, if any**

Often researchers choose to include a subsection on how ethical protocols were ensured while the research was conducted. Institutions such as colleges and universities, as well as funding sources such as government agencies, usually require researchers to first obtain the permission of their institutional ethics board and committees prior to undertaking the research. Once approved, they are likely to require that the researcher obtain informed consent from the individuals who will be participating in their research study. This is done with a consent form. A basic consent form describes the purpose of the study, the possible benefits and harm that might result from participation, and identifies those who are conducting the research. Potential participants are asked to sign the form acknowledging that they freely agree to participate and that they understand that they are free to withdraw from the study at any time without penalty.[3]

Example 9.4.1 illustrates how to briefly describe the use of informed consent in a research report. Note that the authors indicate that all those contacted signed the form. If the rate is less than 100%, the percentage or the number that signed (and, therefore, participated in the research) should be reported.

Example 9.4.1

Participants were 108 undergraduates enrolled in an introductory sociology course. Each was given an informed consent form, which had been approved by the university's institutional review board. The form indicated that (1) the study concerned attitudes toward fully online courses, (2) the students were not required to participate, and (3) if they did participate, they could withdraw from the study at any time without penalty. All students signed the form and participated fully.

When minors are participants, informed consent should be obtained from parents or guardians. This process should be described in the research report. Example 9.4.2 indicates how this might be done.

Example 9.4.2

Interviewers read the consent and assent forms aloud to participants and their guardians, and written parent consent and adolescent assent were obtained from all participants.[4]

> **Guideline 9.5 Consider describing steps taken to maintain confidentiality of the data.**

Participants have the right to expect that the data they provide will remain confidential. Some researchers describe the steps they have taken in order to maintain participant confidentiality, as illustrated in Example 9.5.1.

Example 9.5.1

To protect client confidentiality, our team first ensured that the network was secure. This was done by using a virtual private network (VPN) during the teleconsultation sessions. A VPN is a network that utilizes existing systems of connection (e.g., Internet) to create a private connection between two networks. Within a VPN, two parties can be connected through a private line that is inaccessible to other users. This ensured that the only individuals viewing the information being transferred between the training team and the participants were the relevant parties.[5]

> **Guideline 9.6 The participants should be described in enough detail for the reader to visualize them**

Example 9.6.1 helps readers visualize the participants' gender, experience, institutional affiliation, and racial/ethnic self-identifications. Note that the author points readers to a table that elaborates on the demographics even further; this is common in research reports that track numerous characteristics.

Example 9.6.1

Based on this sampling criteria, I recruited 12 interview participants at the Guiding the Way to Inclusion (GWI) conference hosted by NACAC. The conference was an ideal setting for discussing profiles because the event draws hundreds of admission professionals who are committed to promoting access, equity, and inclusion in the admission process. Following the event, I then used a snowball sampling approach to identify other individuals who did not attend the conference but fit the study's sampling criteria. These respondents provided a counterbalance to the perspectives of the GWI attendees who were heavily invested in this topic and may have expressed stronger opinions as a result. In total, 25 admission professionals from a range of backgrounds were interviewed, representing nine liberal arts colleges and 13 universities. Approximately 60% of participants identified as female and 32% as people of color. Years of experience in the admission field ranged from 2 to 28, with an average of 8.1. Additional information about individual interview participants, including whether they attended GWI, can be found in Table 1.[6]

Because the number of characteristics that might be used to describe participants is almost limitless, researchers should be selective in deciding on which ones to report. As a general rule, describe those that are most relevant to the issues being studied. For instance, in a study on physicians' attitudes toward assisted suicide, "religious background" would be a relevant characteristic. For a study on algebra achievement, it would not be relevant.

➤ Guideline 9.7 Consider reporting demographics in tables

Tables such as the one in Example 9.7.1 make it easy for readers to scan the information that describes the participants. Note the use of the term *demographic characteristics* in the title of the table. These are background characteristics that help readers visualize the participants.

Example 9.7.1

Table 1. Demographic Characteristics of the Participants

Characteristic	Number	Percent
Gender		
Female	81	72
Male	31	28
Current grade level		
Third	16	14
Fourth	37	33
Fifth	55	49
Sixth	4	4
Qualify for subsidized school lunch program?		
Yes	99	88
No	13	12
Family status		
Living with both parents	72	64
Living with one parent	35	31
Living with neither parent	5	4

➤ **Guideline 9.8 When a sample is very small, consider providing a description of individual participants**

The information on a small number of individuals can be presented in a paragraph or in a table, as in Example 9.8.1.

Example 9.8.1

Table 2. Select Demographic Characteristics and Psychiatric Diagnoses of the Participants

Client	Age	Gender	Psychiatric diagnosis
1	19	M	Conduct disorder
			Attention deficit disorder
			Learning disability
2	20	M	Dysthymic disorder
3	20	M	Major depression
4	20	F	Major depression
5	21	M	Conduct disorder
6	22	F	Dysthymic disorder

➤ **Guideline 9.9 If only a sample was studied, the method of sampling should be described**

Sometimes, researchers study entire populations (i.e., the entire sets of individuals in which the researchers are interested). More often, they sample from a population, study the sample, and then generalize (i.e., infer that what is true of the sample is also true of the population).

When sampling is conducted, the researchers should name the population from which the sample was drawn and indicate the method used to draw the sample (e.g., simple random sampling). Example 9.9.1 illustrates how this might be done.

Example 9.9.1

From the population of all registered nurses in public hospitals in Texas, 120 were selected using simple random sampling.

When a researcher draws a sample of convenience (very often students at the college or university where the researcher is employed), this fact should be explicitly mentioned, as in Example 9.9.2.

Example 9.9.2

A convenience sample consisting of 42 women and 34 men participated in this study. All participants were enrolled as students at a large public university in the southwestern United States. The participants were volunteers who responded to an email seeking participants to take part in a study of online gaming habits. The email indicated that the survey would take about 45 minutes and that a $10 Amazon gift card would be sent to each participant.

➤ Guideline 9.10 Explicitly acknowledge weaknesses in sampling

When the method of sampling is clearly deficient, such as the one in Example 9.9.2, it is a good idea for the author to acknowledge this fact with a sentence such as "Because a sample of convenience was used, generalizations to populations should be made with extreme caution," or "The use of volunteers as participants in this study greatly restricts the generalizability of the results." Inclusion of statements such as these is especially important in student projects, theses, and dissertations. In their absence, instructors may not know whether students are aware of this important limitation.[7]

➤ Guideline 9.11 Provide detailed information on nonparticipants when possible

Information on individuals who refuse to participate in a study is often available and usually should be reported. For instance, in a study on achievement in a school setting, the cumulative records of nonparticipating students might be accessed so that average standardized test scores for those who participated and those who declined to participate can be accounted for.

The researcher who wrote Example 9.11.1 recruited participants via social media and personal connections given access challenges during the COVID-19 pandemic. The researcher addressed the limitations of their recruitment methods, as seen in Example 9.11.2.

Example 9.11.1

One hundred eighty-one teachers consented to participate, but 30 participants (16.6%) who did not answer any survey items were removed from the analysis, resulting in a final sample of 151 participants.[8]

Example 9.11.2

Overall, it is of vital importance to be careful when interpreting and generalizing the findings of this study due to the methodological limitations.[9]

➤ **Guideline 9.12 Describe the measures after describing the participants**

Measures are instruments (such as achievement tests, attitude scales, questionnaires, checklists, and interview schedules).

Immediately under the subheading of "Method" (centered in bold) should appear the subheading "Participants" (flush left in bold). The next subheading is "Measures" (flush left in bold). A portion of Example 1.4.1 in Chapter 1 is reproduced here as Example 9.12.1 to show the placement of the material on measures (see the arrow in the example).

Example 9.12.1

Title in Upper- and Lowercase Letters
Abstract (a main heading; centered in bold)
A literature review that introduces the research problem (with no heading)
Method (a main heading; centered in bold)
Participants (a subheading; flush left in bold)
⇨ **Measures** (a subheading; flush left in bold)

➤ **Guideline 9.13 Describe the traits a measure was designed to measure, its format, and the possible range of score values**

Consider Example 9.13.1, which has insufficient detail, and its improved version.

Example 9.13.1

Attitude toward school was measured with a nine-item online survey developed for use in this study.

Improved Version of Example 9.13.1

Attitude toward school was measured with an online survey developed for use in this study. It contains nine statements. The first three measure attitudes toward academic subjects. The next three measure attitudes toward teachers, counselors, and administrators. The last three measure attitudes toward the social environment in the school. Participants were asked to rate each statement on a five-point scale from 1 (strongly disagree) to 5 (strongly agree). Scores for individual participants could range from 9 (strongly disagreeing with all nine statements) to 45 (strongly agreeing with all statements). The complete questionnaire is shown in Appendix A of this journal article.

Notice these desirable characteristics of the improved version of Example 9.13.1: It indicates (1) the number of items, (2) what the items were designed to measure, (3) the scale (i.e., strongly disagree to strongly agree) that was used, (4) the possible range of scores, and (5) the availability of the complete measure. For long instruments, some researchers do not include the entire measure in the research report, but rather make copies available on request.

➤ Guideline 9.14 Summarize information on reliability and validity, when available

The two most important characteristics of a measure are its *reliability* (consistency of results) and *validity* (the extent to which the measure actually measures what it is designed to measure).

For research projects and journal articles, researchers typically provide only brief summaries of what is known about a measure's reliability and validity, as illustrated in Example 9.14.1.

Example 9.14.1

Psychometric evaluations of the OPD-2 showed acceptable-to-good reliability as well as good validity for the individual axes (Cierpka et al., 2007).[10]

In Example 9.14.2, the writers summarize information on internal consistency reliability, test-retest reliability (i.e., stability), as well as validity.

Example 9.14.2

Epworth Sleepiness Scale. Both internal consistency reliability (.73–.88) and stability (r = .82) of the ESS have been established (Johns, 1992), with a reliability of .71 obtained in this study. The ESS has been identified as a valid measure of sleep propensity in adults, with the ability to differentiate between groups known to have varying levels of sleepiness, such as healthy adults and patients with narcolepsy or sleep apnea (Johns, 1994).[11]

Students who are writing theses and dissertations may be expected to describe the reliability and validity of the measures they use in considerable detail. They may be expected, for instance, to summarize how the reliability and validity studies were conducted and to interpret the results of these studies in light of any methodological flaws in the studies.

➤ Guideline 9.15 Provide references where more information on the measures can be found

When there is published information on measures, especially on their reliability and validity, provide references to it. This is illustrated in the last sentences in Examples 9.14.1 and 9.14.2.

➤ Guideline 9.16 Consider providing sample items or questions

It can be helpful to readers to see sample items (such as test items) or questions (such as interview questions). Example 9.16.1 illustrates how this might be done.

Example 9.16.1

The Multidimensional Perfectionism Scale (MPS) is a 45-item scale that assesses the first CMPB trait component with three trait dimensions, namely, *self-oriented perfectionism* (e.g., "When I am working on something, I cannot relax until it is perfect"), *other-oriented perfectionism* (e.g., "I have high expectations for people who are important to me"), and *socially prescribed perfectionism* (e.g., "I feel that people are too demanding of me") using a 7-point scale from 1 (*strongly disagree*) to 7 (*strongly agree*).[12]

➤ **Guideline 9.17 Make unpublished measures available**

Researchers often construct new measures (or modify existing measures) for use in their research. For short measures, consider providing the complete set of items (or questions) in the description of the measure, as is done in Example 9.17.1.

Example 9.17.1

These questions were: (1) Regarding techniques for teaching my child new skills, I feel the individual therapy he/she participated in helped him/her learn … (A) no new skills, (B) a few new skills, (C) some new skills, (D) a reasonable amount of new skills, or (E) many new skills; and (2) Overall, I feel the individual therapy my child participated in was … (A) not at all helpful, (B) a little helpful, (C) somewhat helpful, (D) helpful, or (E) very helpful. Responses to these questions scored between 1 (*not helpful/learned no new skills*) and 5 (*very helpful/learned many new skills*) and summed across both questions for a score ranging between 2 and 10).[13]

For longer measures, consider putting them in a table (instead of providing them in a paragraph) within the subsection on measures. Example 9.17.2 shows a table that was included in a research report. It shows the complete set of questions used in a focus group study.

Example 9.17.2

Table 3. Focus Group Questions[14]

[Q1] "Let's start with the most blatant form of microaggressions, microassaults. Microassaults are when a person says or does something seemingly small to intentionally hurt you. Could you describe a time at work where this has occurred?"

[Q2] "There are more ambiguous forms of microaggressions. There may have been times where you were unsure if the person meant to insult you. For example, in an attempt to compliment you they may have said something offensive. In other instances, they may have made a comment that they were unaware was offensive or insulting. Can you think of situations at work where this has occurred?"

[Q3] "Sometimes people or situations in the workplace may have been dismissive or invalidated your thoughts or feelings [microinvalidations]. Can you think of a case at work that you have experienced?"

[Q4] "Have any of these circumstances at work contributed to your stress? Could you explain how?"

[Q5] "Have these experiences shaped the decisions you have made about your job? This may include the decision to leave your job, change your working hours, or attempt to move to a different position or workplace."

[Q6] "So far we've talked about your different experiences of microaggressions at work and how they have affected your stress and decisions in the workplace. How have these workplace conditions affected your relationships with your coworkers and supervisors?"

[Q7] "Let's focus on what helps you deal with these scenarios. How do you cope?"

For longer measures, an alternative to using a table is to put copies of complete measures in an appendix at the end of the research report. When this is done, mention the appendix in the body of the report, which is illustrated in the last sentence of the improved version of Example 9.13.1.

Concluding Comments

This chapter deals with the two questions almost universally addressed under the main heading of Method: (1) Who were the participants/what was the sample? and (2) What measures were used?

The next chapter deals with special issues in describing the methods used in experiments (i.e., studies in which participants are given treatments in order to observe their responses).

Exercises for Chapter 9

Part A

1. According to this chapter, when is it logical to refer to individuals studied as *participants*?

2. Should a consent form describe both possible benefits and possible harm?

3. Suppose a teacher is writing a research report on the effectiveness of new materials for teaching second-grade math. Name two characteristics of the participants that might be relevant for inclusion in a report on this topic.

4. What are *demographic characteristics*?

5. If a researcher uses a *convenience sample*, should this fact be mentioned in the research report?

6. Is it desirable to provide information on nonparticipants (e.g., those who refuse to participate in a study)?

7. Within the Method section, should "participants" or "measures" be described first?

8. Are researchers who write journal articles expected to describe the reliability and validity of the measures they use in considerable detail?

9. What are the two ways for making long, complete measures available?

Part B

10. Locate a description of participants in a research report in a journal article, thesis, or dissertation that you think lacks sufficient detail. Copy it, and briefly describe other types of information that might have been included to give a better picture of the participants.

11. Locate a description of the measures in a research report in a journal article, thesis, or dissertation that describes its reliability and validity. (Note that some authors use the subheading "Instrumentation" for the section on measures.)

Notes

1   Tomić, Pinćjer, Dedijer, & Adamović (2022, p. 16).
2   Other terms that are sometimes used are *respondents* (e.g., to refer to individuals who respond to an emailed survey) and *examinees* (e.g., to refer to individuals who are participating in test development research). Qualitative researchers sometimes prefer the term *informants*.
3   Precise requirements for preparing an informed consent form should be obtained from the appropriate institution or funding agency.
4   Zhang & Gonzales-Backen (2023, p. 4).
5   Peterson, Eldridge, Rios, & Schenk (2019, p. 193).
6   Nicola (2022, p. 704).
7   While statements regarding generalizing from a sample are often made in the Method section, many researchers also make them in the Discussion section at the end of the research report. See Chapter 12.
8   Chan et al. (2021, p. 535).
9   Ibid. (p. 543).
10 Kadur et al. (2022, p. 848).
11 Scott, Hofmeister, Rogness, & Rogers (2010, pp. 253–254).
12 Hewitt et al. (2023, p. 33).
13 Bushman & Peacock (2010, pp. 108–109).
14 Lee, Ditchman, Thomas, & Tsen (2019, p. 182).

Chapter 10

Describing Experimental Methods

An *experiment* is a study in which treatments are given in order to determine their effects on participants. A set of treatments (e.g., two levels of a drug dosage) is known as the *independent variable*, while the outcome (e.g., feeling less pain) is the *dependent variable*.

➤ **Guideline 10.1 Describe experimental methods under the subheading "Procedure" under the main heading of "Method"**

A portion of Example 1.4.1 in Chapter 1 is reproduced here as Example 10.1.1 to show the placement of the material described in this chapter (see the arrow in the example). Note that the previous chapter describes what to include under "Participants" and "Measures," which are also subheadings under "Method."

Example 10.1.1

Title in Upper- and Lowercase Letters

Abstract (a main heading; centered in bold)[1]

A literature review that introduces the research problem (with no heading)

Method (a main heading; centered in bold)

Participants (a subheading; flush left in bold)

Measures (a subheading; flush left in bold)

⇨ **Procedure** (optional; a subheading; flush left in bold)

DOI: 10.4324/9781003230410-11

➤ **Guideline 10.2 If there are two or more groups, explicitly
state how the groups were formed**

When two or more groups are to be compared (e.g., comparing an experimental
and a control group), random group assignment is highly desirable because it assures
that there was no bias. Example 10.2.1 illustrates how the use of random assignment
might be described.

Example 10.2.1

Randomization of intervention phases was ensured using an electronic sequence
generator.[2]

➤ **Guideline 10.3 Distinguish between *random selection*
and *random assignment***

When selecting individuals to participate in an experiment, it is desirable to select
individuals at random. Whether or not the individuals were selected at random, it
is desirable to assign the selected individuals at random to the comparison groups in
an experiment. Consider Example 10.3.1, in which the researcher indicates that the
selection was random (i.e., classes were selected at random) and that the assignment
was at random (i.e., randomized group assignment was used).

Example 10.3.1

One kindergarten was chosen randomly from each of six educational districts
in the State of Kuwait. Two classes were chosen randomly from each kindergarten; therefore, 12 classes in total participated in the study. The two classes
in each kindergarten were assigned randomly to the two groups of the study,
group A and group B, each of which was divided into six teams.[3]

➤ **Guideline 10.4 For experiments with only one participant,
describe the length of each condition**

In some experiments, only one participant (or only one group of participants) is
used. These are often referred to as *single-subject designs* (also called *behavior analysis*).
In these, it is typical to observe the participant's behavior for a period before any
treatments are administered (this is called the *baseline*), and then alternate treatments
for varying periods. Example 10.4.1 illustrates how such an arrangement might be

described, indicating the length of each condition, including the "reversal," which refers to returning to the original condition (i.e., without treatment).

Example 10.4.1

For baseline data, the infant's parents first recorded the number of night awakenings for seven consecutive nights. During the following seven nights, the parents played a white noise machine [described above], while continuing to record the number of night awakenings. On the 15th and 16th nights, a reversal was instituted with the white noise machine turned off ...

➤ **Guideline 10.5 Describe the experimental treatment in detail**

Without a detailed description, readers will be unable to determine how to administer the treatment in order to get similar results. Often researchers choose to include a subsection on how ethical protocols were ensured while the research was conducted.

In general, it is better to err on the side of providing too much detail than too little detail on experimental treatments. Examples 10.5.1 and 10.5.2 illustrate the degree of detail that might be expected by consumers of research.

Example 10.5.1

An iPad was used to access the application *Learning Touch, First Sight Words Pro* https://itunes.apple.com/us/app/first-sight-words-professional/id515121228?mt=8. This application presented the words selected in the vocabulary list. It included auditory, visual, and kinesthetic approaches for each word presented. For example, an individual word was always presented together with a visual image.[4]

Example 10.5.2

In the final 10 minutes of class, researchers introduced themselves and provided a brief description of the current study's intent to investigate migration patterns in student seating in the CIRS building; however, special effort was made to avoid drawing attention to the impact of seat location and computer use on student performance. The researchers then distributed paper handouts, numbered by seating row, and students were required to indicate their seat number, initials, last five digits of their student number, and Yes or No as to whether or not they used a laptop computer or some other electronic device (e.g., a phone or tablet) for note taking.[5]

➤ Guideline 10.6 Describe physical controls over the administration of the experimental treatment

This guideline is especially applicable to experiments in which colleagues and assistants are used to administer treatments. For instance, a researcher might have graduate students administer experimental counseling. Questions that should be addressed in such a situation are as follows: To what extent were the graduate students trained in the experimental counseling process? What type of supervision was provided for the graduate students? Were there spot-checks to determine if the graduate students were following protocol? Were the graduate students required to keep a log of their efforts to implement the counseling?

➤ Guideline 10.7 Describe the control condition

Describe any conditions under which a control group was held. For instance, was the study conducted fully online (e.g., via Zoom)? Were the control group participants free to go their own way between, before, and after testing? Were they in the same room as the experimental students during the treatment of the experimental group? Were they assigned to do independent study? Varying conditions in the control condition could cause differences in how the control group responds, so the control condition should be described.

➤ Guideline 10.8 Describe steps taken to reduce the "expectancy effect"

When participants are able to determine (or guess) the expected effect of an experiment, they may respond accordingly (e.g., they may behave in the way they believe they are expected to respond). If any steps were taken to reduce this possibility, they should be described. Example 10.8.1 illustrates this guideline.

Example 10.8.1

While the purpose of the experiment was to examine students' attitudes toward female professors of color (e.g., African American, Latinx), the attitude scale touched on a number of issues relating to instruction in higher education in an effort to mask the true purpose of the experiment. Only the 10 items dealing with attitudes toward female professors of color, however, were scored for the purposes of the analysis.

In pharmacological research, the *expectancy effect* is referred to as the *placebo effect*. It is standard procedure in experiments on new drugs to provide the control group with a *placebo* (an inert substance that looks like the experimental drug). To inhibit the expectancy effect, a *blind* procedure is typically used (i.e., the patient does not know whether the medication he or she is receiving is active or inert). In a *double-blind* procedure, neither the patient nor the individual dispensing the medication knows this. When a blind or double-blind procedure is used, it should be described, as illustrated in Example 10.8.2.

Example 10.8.2

A double-blind procedure was used in which neither the patient nor the nurse who was dispensing the medication knew whether the active drug or the placebo was being administered.

> ### Guideline 10.9 If there was attrition, describe the dropouts

This guideline refers to the attrition (i.e., dropping out) of individuals who began to participate in an experiment but dropped out before its conclusion. Attrition can make the interpretation of the results of an experiment difficult whenever there is the possibility that those who dropped out are different from those who remained, or those who dropped out of the experimental group are different from those who dropped out of the control group (called *differential attrition*).

For instance, in a study of an experimental drug, those who dropped out of the experimental group might have done so because they experienced serious side effects. One partial solution to this problem is to ask them the reasons why they dropped out. Unfortunately, sometimes dropouts cannot be located for questioning and some of those who are located may not be cooperative in providing such information.

Because attrition can be an important problem, the demographics and other available information about dropouts should be provided, if possible. Example 10.9.1 illustrates this guideline.

Example 10.9.1

Two boys (ages 10 and 11) and three girls (all age 10) dropped out of the experimental group because their families moved out of the school district. All five were Latinx and spoke English as a second language. Their percentile ranks on the *Metropolitan Reading Test* (English Version) ranged from 45 to 65,

---

> which is similar to the percentile ranks of the participants who did not drop out. None of the students in the control group dropped out.

In simple experiments (e.g., a treatment is given in a short amount of time with few demands on participants), there is likely to be little or no attrition, in which case this issue may not need to be addressed.

➤ Guideline 10.10 If participants were debriefed, mention it

Debriefing consists of informing participants at the end of an experiment of its purposes and allowing participants to ask questions of the researchers. While informed consent forms provide general statements of purposes, debriefing describes the purposes in more detail. This process is described in Example 10.10.1.

Example 10.10.1

Structured debriefs follow each simulation to explore reactions, 'unpicking' actual events with a focus on how learning transfers to the real workplace. Facilitators strive to cultivate a safe and positive atmosphere during debriefing with emphasis on transfer or learning of future-focused principles and practices.[6]

Debriefing is especially important in experiments in which the specific purposes were not described in the consent form, which is often done to reduce the *expectancy effect* (see Guideline 10.8). Describing debriefing assures readers that participants' rights to knowledge of the full purposes of an experiment were protected.

Exercises for Chapter 10

Part A

1. Should experimental procedures be described before *or* after measures?

2. Does the following statement describe "random selection" *or* "random assignment"? "From the entire population of 224 sixth graders, 50 were identified at random to participate in the experiment."

3. What is a baseline?

4. Should the length of a baseline be described?

5. Without a detailed description of the experimental treatment, readers will be unable to determine what?

6. Which guideline is especially applicable to experiments in which colleagues and assistants are used to administer treatments?

7. Is it ever desirable to describe the control condition?

8. Briefly define the *expectancy effect*.

9. What is the name of the problem that refers to individuals dropping out of an experiment?

Part B

Examine a report of an experiment published in a peer-reviewed journal and answer the following questions.

10. If there was more than one group in the experiment, was the basis for assignment to groups clearly described? Explain.

11. Was the experimental treatment described in sufficient detail? Explain.

12. Was the topic of attrition addressed? If so, summarize what was said.

Notes

1 This heading should usually be used in unpublished papers. In research journals, it is often omitted, with the abstract being identified by its placement at the beginning and by being indented on the left and right.
2 Ritter, Morrison, & Sherman (2021, p. 565).
3 Dashti & Habeeb (2020, p. 524).
4 Xin & Affrunti (2019, p. 74).
5 Will, Bischof, & Kingstone (2020, p. 5).
6 Jowsey et al. (2020, p. 4).

Chapter 11

Writing Analysis and Results Sections

While the Analysis subsection and the Results section typically are separate sections of a research report, they are closely aligned and are covered together in this chapter.

> ### Guideline 11.1 "Analysis" is a subheading under the main heading of "Method"[1]

A portion of Example 1.4.1 in Chapter 1 is reproduced below as Example 11.1.1 to show the placement of the material on Analysis (see the arrow in the example).

Example 11.1.1

Title in Upper- and Lowercase Letters
Abstract (a main heading; centered in bold)
A literature review that introduces the research problem (with no heading)
Method (a main heading; centered in bold)
Participants (a subheading; flush left in bold)
Measures (a subheading; flush left in bold)
Procedure (optional; a subheading; flush left in bold)
⇨ **Analysis** (optional; a subheading; flush left in bold)

> ### Guideline 11.2 The Analysis subsection is used sparingly in reports on quantitative research

If straightforward, widely recognized methods of statistical analysis were used to analyze the data, the subsection on analysis may be omitted in reports of quantitative research.

 DOI: 10.4324/9781003230410-12

Quantitative researchers are likely to include a subsection on analysis if they have used advanced statistical methods that may not be familiar to their readers. Example 11.2.1 shows a portion of the Analysis subsection in which an advanced method is described.

Example 11.2.1

We used analysis of variance (ANOVA) to assess relationships among informal education and professional development and the six knowledge dimensions.[2]

➤ Guideline 11.3 The Analysis subsection is usually included in reports on qualitative research

Because there are many approaches to the analysis of qualitative data (e.g., transcripts from interviews), the approach selected for a particular research project should be named and briefly described, which is illustrated in Examples 11.3.1 and 11.3.2— each of which is a portion of the subsection on analysis in a report on qualitative research. Notice that the researchers provide references where more information on the method of analysis can be obtained.

Example 11.3.1

Focus groups were recorded and transcribed, and data were analysed manually using thematic analysis (Green and Thorogood, 2014). This four-stage analysis, accessible to the researchers, offered flexibility (Nowell et al, 2017). Analysis, coding of transcripts and theme identification had an audit trail for transparency.[3]

Example 11.3.2

Analysis of the qualitative data was done using MAXQDA 2022. Thematic analysis was used to analyze the verbatim transcripts of the focus groups, following the steps described by Braun and Clarke: 1) becoming familiar with the data, 2) generating initial codes, 3) searching for themes, 4) reviewing them, 5) defining and naming themes, and 6) producing the report.[4]

> ## Guideline 11.4 "Results" is a main heading that follows the main heading "Method"

Portions of Examples 1.4.1 and 1.7.1 in Chapter 1 are reproduced below as Example 11.4.1 to show the placement of the results (see the arrow in the example).

Example 11.4.1

Title in Upper- and Lowercase Letters

Abstract (a main heading; centered in bold)

A literature review that introduces the research problem (with no heading)

Method (a main heading; centered in bold)

Participants (a subheading; flush left in bold)

Measures (a subheading; flush left in bold)

Procedure (optional; a subheading; flush left in bold)

Analysis (optional; a subheading; flush left in bold)

⇨ **Results** (a main heading; centered in bold)

> ## Guideline 11.5 Organize the Results section around the research hypotheses, objectives, or questions

This guideline helps readers understand the organization of the results. Example 11.5.1 shows the three research questions posed near the beginning of the report. It also shows a portion of the results. Notice how the results are organized around the three research questions.

Example 11.5.1

Research questions posed near the beginning of the report

Specifically, three questions guided this research: (a) Is parental involvement associated with program effectiveness in terms of students' achievement? (b) Is parental involvement associated with attendance rates? and (c) Is parental involvement associated with their children's desire to continue to take part in the program?

Portions of the Results section, which illustrate the organization around the three research questions

The first research question concerned the possible association between parental involvement and students' achievement. Table 1 shows the means

---

and standard deviations on three achievement tests for two groups of students: students whose parents were highly involved and students whose parents were less involved. A statistically significant difference was found between ...

To examine the second research question, parents' scores on the involvement scale were correlated with their children's attendance in program sessions. Specifically, the involvement scores were correlated with number of days attended. This analysis indicated that parents' involvement was significantly correlated with ...

The third research question concerned the association between parental involvement and children's desire to continue to take part in the program. The analysis of the data on this question revealed ...

➤ **Guideline 11.6 It is usually not necessary to show formulas or calculations in either the Analysis or Results sections**

Formulas and calculations for widely used statistics do not need to be shown in research reports. In addition, it is usually unnecessary to name the software used (e.g., Excel) to perform the analysis.

➤ **Guideline 11.7 The scores of individual participants usually are not shown**

Suppose a random sample of 50 students in an elementary school was tested with a standardized achievement test battery. Normally, a researcher would *not* list the scores of individual children. Instead, the researcher would provide summary statistics such as the mean and standard deviation. Note, however, that some instructors may require students who are writing term projects, theses, and dissertations to include participants' scores in an appendix so that the instructor can check the analysis.

➤ **Guideline 11.8 Present descriptive statistics before inferential statistics**

For each set of scores, provide information on central tendency and variability (usually means and standard deviations), then present correlation coefficients, if any. Finally, present the results of inferential statistical tests such as the *t* test.

For categorical (nominal) data, present frequencies and percentages before presenting the results of inferential statistical tests such as the chi-square test.

➤ Guideline 11.9 Organize large numbers of statistics in tables or other visuals

Tables and visuals are especially effective for helping readers compare groups and visualize data. The table in Example 11.9.1 makes it easy to compare the ages of women and men.

Example 11.9.1

Table 1. *Percentage and Number of Women and Men in Various Age Groups*

Age	Women (n = 830)	Men (n = 723)
18 years and under	4.8% (*n* = 40)	8.7% (*n* = 63)
19–24 years	9.9% (*n* = 82)	13.3% (*n* = 96)
25–34 years	18.2% (*n* = 151)	25.4% (*n* = 184)
35–44 years	22.8% (*n* = 189)	19.4% (*n* = 140)
45–54 years	20.0% (*n* = 166)	15.4% (*n* = 111)
55–64 years	13.7% (*n* = 114)	13.8% (*n* = 100)
65–74 years	5.3% (*n* = 44)	2.6% (*n* = 19)
75 years and over	5.3% (*n* = 44)	1.4% (*n* = 10)
Total	100.0%	100.0%

➤ Guideline 11.10 Give each table or visual a number and a caption (i.e., a descriptive title)

In Example 11.9.1, the Table is numbered "Table 1" and has this caption: *Percentage and Number of Women and Men in Various Age Groups*.

Note that the captions should usually name the statistics presented in the table and the variables studied. Example 11.10.1 shows four titles that do this. For instance, in the first caption in this example, the statistics are number and percentage, while the variables are marital status and welfare status.

Example 11.10.1

Table 1. *Number and Percentage of Participants by Marital Status and Welfare Status*
Table 2. *Means and Standard Deviations on Reading and Mathematics*
Table 3. *Intercorrelation Matrix for Voting-Behavior Variables*
Table 4. *Analysis of Variance for Mathematics Scores*

When separate tables are presented for two or more groups, the title of each table should also name the group. Example 11.10.2 shows the titles of tables for two different groups.

Example 11.10.2

Table 1. *Intercorrelation Matrix of Middle-Level Managers' Personality Scores*
Table 2. *Intercorrelation Matrix of Chief Executive Officers' Personality Scores*

➤ **Guideline 11.11 Refer to statistical tables or visuals by number within the text of the Results section**

Each statistical table included in a report should be referred to in the text by its number (e.g., "Table 1 presents the means and standard deviations for the adolescents"). Note that tables should usually be inserted in research reports *after* the first mention of them.[5]

➤ **Guideline 11.12 When describing the statistics presented in a table or visual, point out only the highlights**

Briefly describe the highlights of each table presented in the Results section. Because the values of the statistics are presented in a table, it is not necessary to repeat each value in the description of the results. This is illustrated in Example 11.12.1, which shows a statistical table, and Example 11.12.2, which shows the discussion of it. Note that in the discussion, only certain specific statistics are mentioned in order to assist the reader in getting an overview of the tabled results.

Example 11.12.1

Table 2. Percentage of Substance Use in Past Month of Urban and Suburban Samples

	Drug A		Drug B		Drug C	
Grade	Urban	Suburban	Urban	Suburban	Urban	Suburban
11	33.6	23.2	13.1	14.0	5.2	4.3
12	34.2	24.1	13.9	13.8	4.7	4.8

Example 11.12.2

Table 1 shows the percentage of urban and suburban 11th and 12th graders who reported using three illicit drugs during the previous month. Overall, Drug A had the highest percentages reporting its use, with percentages for subgroups ranging from 23.2% to 34.2%. Use of Drug B was reported by much smaller percentages of students (from 13.1% to 14.0% for subgroups). Use of Drug C was reported by relatively small percentages of students, with the highest percentage being 5.2% for urban 11th graders. Consistent with the hypothesis, the most striking difference between urban and suburban students was in the reported usage of Drug A, with higher percentages of urban students than suburban students reporting its use.

➤ Guideline 11.13 Figures (e.g., flow charts, graphs, etc.) should be used sparingly

Figures may be used to organize and describe data. They usually take up more space, however, than would a corresponding statistical table. Because space in journals is limited, figures should be used more sparingly than statistical tables. In term projects, theses, and dissertations, where space is not an issue, they may be used more frequently.

Because figures attract the eye better than tables, their best use is to present important data, especially striking data that might otherwise be overlooked in a table of statistical values. Example 11.13.1 shows such a figure, which illustrates a striking difference between the experimental groups and the control group on a scale from zero (no improvement) to 50 (outstanding improvement).

Like statistical tables, statistical figures should be numbered and given captions (titles) that name the variables and the statistics presented, which is done in the following example. Typically, figure numbers and titles are placed *below* the figures. For tables, they are placed *above*. Compare the placement of the caption in the table in Example 11.12.1 (i.e., *Percentage of Substance Use in* …) with the placement of the caption in the figure in Example 11.13.1 (i.e., Mean Improvement Scores for …).[6]

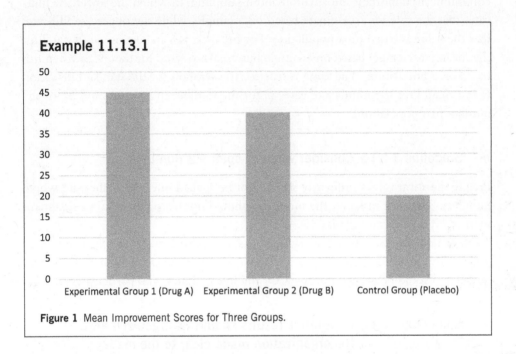

Example 11.13.1

Figure 1 Mean Improvement Scores for Three Groups.

> ## Guideline 11.14 Statistical symbols should be underlined or italicized

In Example 11.14.1, the statistical symbols (i.e., *t*, *df*, and *p*) are italicized. Without italics, "p" is just the letter "p." With italics, *p* is a statistical symbol that stands for *probability*.

Example 11.14.1

The mean of the experimental group was significantly higher than the mean of the control group ($t = 2.310$, $df = 10$, $p < .05$, two-tailed).

> ## Guideline 11.15 Use the proper case for each statistical symbol

As statistical symbols, upper- and lowercase italicized letters often stand for entirely different statistics. For instance, a lowercase *f* stands for *frequency*, while an uppercase *F* is an inferential statistic used in significance testing. Also, a lowercase *t* is the symbol for a statistic frequently used to test the difference between two means, while an uppercase *T* is a special type of standardized test score.

For some statistics, the upper- and lowercases stand for the same statistic but communicate important information about sampling, in which the lowercase indicates that the value is an estimate based on a sample, while the uppercase indicates that the value is based on a population. For instance, researchers use *m* to stand for the mean (an average) based on a sample but use *M* to stand for the mean when it is based on a population. The same is true for the symbols for the standard deviation (*s* and *S*) and for the number of cases (*n* for the number in a sample and *N* for the number in a population).[7]

➤ Guideline 11.16 Consider when to spell out numbers

Precise statistical values ordinarily should not be spelled out even if they are whole numbers. Thus, for instance, the number 8 should not be spelled out in a statement such as: "The median age was 8."

Note that numbers that start sentences should ordinarily be spelled out (e.g., Twenty-five students participated …). Also, whole numbers less than 10 within sentences should be spelled out (e.g., Of the five children who participated …).

➤ Guideline 11.17 Qualitative results should be organized and the organization made clear to the reader

In qualitative studies, statistics are usually not reported. Instead, researchers report on major trends and themes that emerged from subjective and objective analyses of data such as transcribed interviews. The presentation of such results should be organized. To do this, consider using subheadings to guide the reader through the results. This is illustrated in Example 11.17.1, which is the first paragraph in the Results section of a report on a qualitative study. Note that it provides readers with a description of the organization of the results. The remaining portion of the results (not shown in the example) is divided into three parts with subheadings suggested in the example (e.g., Competition and judgement is demotivating).

Example 11.17.1

The adolescents talked about barriers, pros, cons, and possibilities to be physically active. The analysis revealed three themes and six subthemes, see Table 2.[8]

See Chapter 14 for additional information on reporting the results of qualitative research.

Exercises for Chapter 11

Part A

1. According to this chapter, is the Analysis subsection more likely to appear in reports of "quantitative research" or in reports of "qualitative research"?

2. Is Results a "subheading" or a "main heading"?

3. "In the Results section, it is important to show all formulas and calculations." Is this statement true or false?

4. Should "descriptive statistics" or "inferential statistics" be presented first?

5. The captions for tables should usually name what two things?

6. Should all the values in statistical tables be mentioned in the narrative of the Results section? Explain.

7. According to this chapter, are "statistical tables" or "statistical figures" more common in research reports published in journals?

8. How does "p" differ from p in terms of their meanings?

9. How does n differ from N in terms of their meanings?

10. What is incorrect in the following statement? "Initially, there were 60 children in the control group. 15 of these children dropped out of the study."

Part B

11. Examine the Results sections of a quantitative research report published in a journal. List the guidelines in this chapter that were followed by the researcher.

12. Locate a statistical table in a published article that you think has a good title (i.e., caption).

Notes

1 Some writers prefer to place the Analysis subheading immediately under the main heading of Results.
2 Mullikin et al. (2021, p. 513).
3 Coates & Macfadyen (2021, p. 903).
4 Da Rocha Rodrigues et al. (2023, pp. 4–5).
5 In reports being submitted for publication, tables should be included at the end of the report so that the publisher can insert them at appropriate points when the reports are formatted for publication. Some instructors may prefer that students also do this in term-project research reports.

6 Note that in American Psychological Association style, captions for table names are italicized, while captions for figure names are not italicized.

7 Symbols used for the mean and standard deviation may vary among researchers. Because statistics textbooks often use X-bar (an X with a bar over it) as the symbol for the mean, a small percentage of researchers use it instead of m or M in their research reports. In addition, some researchers prefer to use sd and SD instead of s or S as the symbol for the standard deviation.

8 Mikaelsson, Rutberg, Lindqvist, & Michaelson (2020, p. 193).

Chapter 12

Writing Discussion Sections

This chapter presents guidelines for writing the last section of a research report in a journal article or the last chapter of a thesis or dissertation. This section typically begins with one of various headings such as "Summary and Discussion," "Discussion and Conclusions," "Conclusions and Implications," or simply "Discussion."

➤ **Guideline 12.1 "Discussion" is a main heading that follows the main heading "Results"**

Example 12.1.1 shows the placement of the Discussion section relative to the other parts of a research report discussed up to this point in this book (see the arrow in the example).

Example 12.1.1

Title in Upper- and Lowercase Letters
Abstract (a main heading; centered in bold)
A literature review that introduces the research problem (with no heading)
Method (a main heading; centered in bold)
Participants (a subheading; flush left in bold)
Measures (a subheading; flush left in bold)
Procedure (optional; a subheading; flush left in bold)
Analysis (optional; a subheading; flush left in bold)
Results (a main heading; centered in bold)
⇨ **Discussion** (a main heading; centered in bold)

DOI: 10.4324/9781003230410-13

➤ Guideline 12.2 Consider starting the Discussion with a summary

Authors of long research reports, theses, and dissertations often begin their Discussion section with a summary of the highlights of the material that preceded it. The Discussion is not intended to restate all the results that have been presented, rather it should just highlight key findings. For short reports, a summary is not usually necessary.

➤ Guideline 12.3 Early in the Discussion section, refer to the research hypotheses, objectives, or questions

Briefly restate the hypotheses, objectives, or questions and indicate whether the data support the hypotheses, whether the research objectives were achieved, or what answers were obtained for the research questions. This is illustrated in Example 12.3.1, which is the beginning of the Discussion section.

Example 12.3.1

This study sought to explore how former dually-involved youth make sense of their experiences in the foster care and juvenile justice systems, and what they consider to be the unique challenges of being dual-status.[1]

Following this guideline helps to refocus readers' attention on the fundamental purposes of the research report and sets the stage for other aspects of the discussion.

➤ Guideline 12.4 Point out whether results of the current study are consistent with the literature described in the literature review

Because the review of the literature near the beginning of a research report helps set the stage for the current study, it is important to discuss at the end how the current findings relate to those reported earlier in the literature review.

Examples 12.4.1 and 12.4.2 illustrate this guideline.

Example 12.4.1

While three themes emerged from participant responses, the experiences of each was personal, unique, and reflected the extant literature on dual-status and crossover youth.[2]

Example 12.4.2

This research contributes to the existing literature by adding new insights into couples' experiences when raising a young child on the autism spectrum and providing recommendations for clinical practice.[3]

> ### Guideline 12.5 Interpret the results and offer explanations for them in the Discussion section

Following this guideline helps readers understand the results and put them in context. Because interpretations and explanations go beyond the data actually collected, researchers should be careful not to imply that they are data-based explanations. Instead, they are possible explanations that are consistent with the data. The authors of Example 12.5.1 offer an explanation of their findings.

Example 12.5.1

It is interesting to speculate on possible reasons why the fear levels expressed by the 10-year-old children were so much greater than those expressed by the 8-year-old children in this study. One possibility is that the younger children did not have the conceptual background to fully understand the presentation made in the experimental setting. Specifically, they might have ...

It is especially desirable to offer possible explanations for unexpected findings. In Example 12.5.2, the researchers offer an explanation for the finding that responses differed based on the participants' role within an organization (i.e., administrator versus on-the-front-lines service-delivery person).

Example 12.5.2

The central distinction in these responses seemed to be that the on-the-front-lines people generated responses that were more likely to be coded as structural barriers and the administrative-level people generated responses that were more likely to be coded as cognitive affective.[4]

➤ Guideline 12.6 Mention important strengths and limitations in the Discussion section

Strengths and limitations of the research methodology are sometimes first mentioned in the Introduction or the section on methods. Because strengths and limitations can affect the interpretations of data covered in the Discussion section, it is usually appropriate to mention the most important ones in the Discussion section. The authors of Example 12.6.1 point out some strengths of their study. By pointing out that a study is especially strong methodologically, researchers encourage their readers to give more credence to their study, which is important if there are conflicting conclusions reached in weaker studies.

Example 12.6.1

Our study also has several strengths. We had laboratory-quality measurements brought to an everyday school environment. All students had an equal opportunity to participate during the day, and participation was not limited or influenced by, for example, parental motivation to visit a clinic. As we had the unique opportunity to record physiological reactivity in a familiar environment, we gained information beyond laboratory conditions on stressful situations that children and adolescents may experience during their school day. This was also the first study in the field of psychophysiological measurement to include a follow-up past the immediate postintervention assessments.[5]

Example 12.6.2 shows a statement regarding the limitations of a study. A frank discussion of limitations helps warn readers to be cautious in drawing conclusions from a study.

Example 12.6.2

Finally, this study is also limited by the means in which participants were recruited; through purposeful, convenience sampling (Creswell, 2013).[6]

Students who are writing theses and dissertations should provide detailed descriptions of the limitations of their research. Such statements will help to reassure their committee members that the students are knowledgeable of important methodological issues in their research. Students who are writing research reports as term projects should determine how detailed their professors want their discussions of limitations to be.

See Chapter 8 for an additional discussion of writing about strengths and limitations.

➤ **Guideline 12.7 It is usually inappropriate to introduce new data
    or new references in the Discussion section**

The Discussion section of a research report should be used to summarize and interpret what was presented earlier. The introduction of new data or references distracts
from this purpose.

➤ **Guideline 12.8 State specific implications in the Discussion section**

Many academics refer to this point as the "so what?" question. It is important to articulate the importance of the research, even if it suggests that nothing should change. The
"so what?" question should be addressed in the Discussion section and should "sell" the
importance of the study to the reader. If there is a potential for the study to have bigger
implications, it is stated in the form of actions that individuals or organizations should
take based on the results of the study. This is illustrated in Examples 12.8.1 and 12.8.2.

Example 12.8.1

Such a proposition has implications for the content validity of autism knowledge scales, which are largely based on the American Psychiatric Association's
medical criteria for autism as set out in the Diagnostic Statistical Manual
(Harrison et al., 2017a).[7]

Example 12.8.2

Beyond the aforementioned research implications, the findings from this
meta-synthesis have implications for policy, personnel preparation, and practice. Because there are already recommendations for how to make the transition effective and less stressful for young children with disabilities/delays and
their families the field should concentrate their efforts toward making systemic
changes to improve family experiences before, during, and after the transition.
Specifically, additional policies should be put in place to guide, monitor, and
evaluate the transition process and all practitioners should receive additional
training (during personnel preparation programs and professional development
activities) about recommended practices and strategies for successful transition.[8]

In the discussion of the results of pilot studies, researchers often hedge in their statements of implications by beginning them with a caution such as the one shown in
Example 12.8.3.

Example 12.8.3

If the results obtained in this pilot study are confirmed in more definitive studies, the following implications should be considered by ...

➤ **Guideline 12.9 Be specific when making recommendations for future research**

It is uninformative to end a research report with a vague statement such as "Further research is needed." Instead, researchers should point out what specific directions this research might take in order to advance knowledge of a topic. Examples 12.9.1 and 12.9.2 illustrate the degree of specificity often found in research reports published in journal articles.

Example 12.9.1

Given the lack of overall research in the area of EI to ECSE transition, it is clear that additional research is needed, specifically future research should explore the experiences of fathers and families from diverse backgrounds so that we might provide transition services that meet the needs of all families.[9]

Example 12.9.2

The lack of comparable findings across studies of ROOTS also suggest interesting directions for future research addressing how contextual factors affect interactions among different tiers of support and decisions about matching supports to student needs. For example, the null findings here suggest that in a lower-risk sample, when strong core instructional practices are in place, implementing an intensive Tier 2 intervention, such as ROOTS, may not be the best course of action to meet the learning needs of at-risk students.[10]

Note that students who are writing a thesis or dissertation might be expected to discuss suggestions for future research in more detail than shown in Examples 12.9.1 and 12.9.2.

> **Guideline 12.10 Consider using subheadings within the Discussion section**

In a long Discussion section, subheadings can help readers follow the discussion. Example 12.10.1 shows some subheadings that might be used.

Example 12.10.1

        Discussion (a main heading; centered in bold)
Summary (optional; a subheading; flush left in bold)
Strengths of the Current Study (optional; a subheading; flush left in bold)
Limitations (optional; a subheading; flush left in bold)
Implications (optional; a subheading; flush left in bold)
Directions for Future Research (optional; a subheading; flush left in bold)

Exercises for Chapter 12

Part A

1. Is Discussion a "main heading" or a "subheading"?

2. According to this chapter, should a Discussion always begin with a summary? Explain.

3. "Research hypotheses, objectives, and questions should never be repeated in the Discussion section." Is this statement true or false?

4. Should writers refer to the literature cited at the beginning of their reports in their Discussion sections? Why or why not?

5. Is it acceptable for researchers to offer explanations for their results that go beyond the data actually analyzed?

6. Is it usually appropriate to introduce new references in the Discussion section of a research report?

7. Is it appropriate for researchers to describe possible implications of their results *or* should they just restrict themselves to an objective discussion of the actual data?

8. According to this chapter, is it appropriate to end a research report with only this sentence: "Further research is needed"? Explain.

Part B

9. Read a research article published in a journal, thesis, or dissertation, and examine the Discussion section to answer the following questions.

   A. Does the researcher discuss the consistency of the results with previously published results?

   B. Does the researcher mention important strengths and limitations of the current study?

   C. Does the researcher explicitly state the implications of the results?

   D. Does the researcher use subheadings under the main heading of Discussion? If yes, what subheadings were used?

Notes

1 Simmons-Horton (2021, p. 594).
2 Ibid.
3 Downes et al. (2021, p. 2706).
4 Borelli et al. (2022, p. 125).
5 Lassander et al. (2022, pp. 314–315).
6 Martinez, Vega, & Marquez (2019, p. 33).
7 Vincent & Ralston (2020, p. 212).
8 Douglas, Meadan, & Schultheiss (2022, p. 381).
9 Ibid.
10 Clarke et al. (2022, p. 55).

Chapter 13

Writing Abstracts

An *abstract* is a summary of the report. It is placed below the title in a journal article. In a thesis or dissertation, it is usually placed on a separate page following the title page.

➤ **Guideline 13.1 Determine the maximum length permissible for an abstract**

For journals, abstracts are often limited to 250 words or less. For theses, dissertations, and term projects, the word limit may be more generous. In either case, an abstract should be short enough to allow readers to conduct a quick read to determine if the research report will be of interest to them.

➤ **Guideline 13.2 If space permits, consider beginning an abstract by describing the general problem area**

The format of the abstract is often dictated by the journal. However, researchers often begin their abstracts with a brief statement regarding the importance of the problem area. Example 13.2.1 shows the beginning of an abstract that follows this guideline.

Example 13.2.1

Many within the early childhood education community are examining how these changes impact stakeholders' conceptions of school readiness. Yet, little has been done to examine how these same stakeholders make sense of the changed practices of kindergarten itself – the program for which children are getting ready.[1]

DOI: 10.4324/9781003230410-14   127

> ## Guideline 13.3 If space is limited, consider beginning by summarizing the research hypotheses, objectives, or questions

When space is limited, it is best to begin with a statement (or summary) of the research hypotheses, objectives, or questions. Examples 13.3.1 and 13.3.2 show abstracts that follow this guideline.

Example 13.3.1

The purpose of this study is to explore the stressors and coping strategies of single parents during the COVID-19 pandemic, with a focus on social support as a coping strategy.[2]

Example 13.3.2

The main purpose of this study is to analyze and summarize how the three major music teaching methods are implemented in the music classroom for autistic children and how they can help autistic children with different characteristics.[3]

Many researchers indicate their purpose without using the terms *hypothesis*, *objective*, *purpose*, or *question*, which is acceptable. For instance, Example 13.3.3 shows the first sentence of an abstract. It is clear from the sentence that the objective of the study was to evaluate success factors.

Example 13.3.3

The present study investigates and identifies the factors that contribute to the academic success of African American males in a historically Black university.[4]

> ## Guideline 13.4 Highlights of the methodology should be summarized

Information on methodology (such as how variables were measured or what treatments were given in an experiment) helps potential readers determine whether the report will be of interest to them.

Example 13.4.1

We used a concurrent nested approach to mixed methods phenomenological research (QUAN + PHEN) with a survey of a national sample of music teacher educators (N=142) and a phenomenology built from a three-interview series with individuals (n=6) at various career stages.[5]

Example 13.5.1 shows the beginning of an abstract. Notice that the first sentence describes the purpose, while the second and third sentences summarize the research methods used.

➤ **Guideline 13.5 Highlights of the results should be included**

Example 13.5.1 shows a complete abstract. Notice that the abstract starts with the research purpose. Next, it summarizes the research methods. Then, there is a summary of the results. This arrangement is recommended for a short abstract.

Example 13.5.1

The purpose of this study is to explore the experiences of primary pre-service teachers engaged in a peer-group mentoring program during a professional experience placement. Pre-service teachers completed weekly questionnaires and an interview about their experiences. Questionnaire and interview responses were coded and analysed according to three domains of teacher development: professional, personal and social. Common themes about the participants' peer-group mentoring experiences include the role of the professional standards, the practical nature of the activities increased confidence to teach and feelings of belonging and being supported. However, pre-service teachers did not make links between theory and practice in the sessions. This study provides insights into how the Finnish model of peer-group mentoring might be implemented for pre-service teachers in an Australian context.[6]

➤ **Guideline 13.6 Point out any unexpected results**

Unexpected results can lead to advancement of knowledge by stimulating further research to help understand such results. Thus, unexpected results should be pointed out in an abstract, as illustrated in Example 13.6.1.

Example 13.6.1

Unexpectedly, tweets related to Harris were more positive in average sentiment than those regarding Pence.[7]

➤ **Guideline 13.7 If a study is strongly tied to a theory,**
name the theory in the abstract

Typically, theories provide principles that help explain a wide variety of observations. For instance, social learning theory applies to a large number of phenomena
observed in teaching and learning studies.

When the results of individual studies are consistent with predictions based on a
theory, they lend support to the theory. On the other hand, when results of individual studies are inconsistent with a theory, that theory, or at least portions of it,
might need to be reconsidered.

Because of the importance of theories in advancing knowledge, they are sometimes mentioned in the titles of research articles. More often, they are mentioned
in the abstracts. Examples 13.7.1 and 13.7.2 show complete abstracts and illustrate
how to follow this guideline.

Example 13.7.1

Socioemotional selectivity theory postulates that a person with an expansive
future time perspective adopts positive and negative information equally to
prepare for future events, whereas a person with a limited future time perspective favors selecting positive over negative information, which suggests an
information processing bias. Therefore, the present study was conducted to
examine both whether future mental imagery can affect future time perspectives and whether attentional biases can be observed under manipulated future
time perspective conditions. To control for depressive tendencies, which was
assumed to affect the examination of attentional bias, 24 college students with
high depressive tendencies [6 men, 18 women; mean age 18.46 years, standard deviation (SD)=0.66] and 22 with low depressive tendencies (7 men, 15
women; mean age=18.73 years, SD=1.12) were recruited as participants and
instructed to generate mental imagery about the longterm (short-term) future
in order to achieve a limited (expansive) future time perspective condition.
Attentional bias was then examined using an exogenous cueing task with long
cue presentations. The effectiveness of the manipulation method used in this

---

study was confirmed, and the results of the effects on attentional biases were analyzed. A significant difference in the difficulty of attentional disengagement from negative stimuli was observed among the participants with high depressive tendencies under the expansive future time perspective condition.[8]

Example 13.7.2

Older adults are at an elevated risk for passive suicide ideation. The interpersonal theory of suicide and the 3-step theory may provide a framework to better understand factors that contribute to passive suicide ideation among older adults. Specifically, this study aimed to test components of prominent suicide theories and examine the role of meaning in life in the associations between hopelessness, thwarted belongingness, perceived burdensomeness and passive suicide ideation among older adults. Participants were 243 adults aged 60 and older recruited from primary care settings in the southwest United States. We hypothesized that high meaning in life would weaken the associations between hopelessness, thwarted belongingness, perceived burdensomeness and passive suicide ideation. Results from moderation analyses indicate that meaning in life was a significant moderator of the associations between hopelessness and passive suicide ideation, thwarted belongingness and passive suicide ideation, and perceived burdensomeness and passive suicide ideation. These findings suggest that when meaning in life is low there are significant negative associations between hopelessness, thwarted belongingness, perceived burdensomeness and passive suicide ideation among older adults. Implications, limitations, and future directions are discussed.[9]

➤ Guideline 13.8 Mention any unique aspects of a study

Elements that make a research study unique should be mentioned in an abstract. For instance, if a study is the first true experiment (e.g., an experiment with randomization) on a particular problem, this unique aspect should be pointed out in the abstract.

➤ Guideline 13.9 Mention if a line of inquiry is new

Individuals often review abstracts to identify new ways of working with problems. If the line of inquiry is new, its newness should be pointed out in an abstract, as illustrated in Example 13.9.1 (italics added for emphasis).

Example 13.9.1

The 2017 reform of the Swedish national curriculum requires that all compulsory school mathematics and technology teachers integrate programming into their teaching. The new programming policy poses a particular challenge since a majority of the affected teachers have little or no previous programming experience. This paper reports on a study of teachers preparing to implement the *new policy*. Insight into the preparation process was made possible through recorded group conversations and data were collected in March 2018, less than 4 months before the formal enactment of the *new curriculum*. The results, conceptualised by using a framework for intrinsic and extrinsic challenges, reveal several challenges that can potentially affect the uptake of the programming policy and the quality of implementation such as uncertainty about the subject content, unequal professional development opportunities, lack of teaching materials and recurring problems with school IT infrastructure. This study seeks to provide knowledge about teachers' concerns and expressed needs while negotiating programming as new curriculum content and thus aims to contribute to the understanding of teachers' strategies to approach the 2017 Swedish educational reform that introduces programming. Such knowledge is valuable for the possibilities to better understand under what circumstances programming is included in school mathematics and technology. The results illustrate the complexity of curriculum reform implementation and may be of value for decision makers at all levels of school policy and also for providers of both in-service and preservice teacher training.[10]

➤ **Guideline 13.10 If implications and suggestions for future research are emphasized in the report, consider concluding the abstract by mentioning them**

This guideline applies when the Discussion section of a report describes important implications and/or explicit suggestions for future research. In contrast, if these elements are mentioned only in passing, they should not be mentioned in an abstract.

Notice the last sentence in the abstract in Example 13.9.1, which refers to implications.

➤ **Guideline 13.11 An abstract should usually be short; however, there are exceptions**

Many journals limit the word count of their abstracts—some as short as 250 words or less. Journals published by the American Psychological Association limit abstracts to a maximum of 150 to 250 words, depending on the journal. Example 13.11.1 shows the suggested organization for a short abstract.

Example 13.11.1

Suggested elements to cover in a short abstract (no subheadings)

1. Research hypotheses, purposes, or questions. These may need to be abbreviated or summarized if they are extensive.
2. Highlights of the research methods.
3. Highlights of the results.

Students who are writing theses and dissertations should determine their institution's requirements regarding length and number of words. When long abstracts are permitted (or required), consider incorporating information on the importance of the problem and the implications of the results in addition to the other elements mentioned in the earlier guidelines in this chapter. Example 13.11.2 shows the suggested organization for a long abstract.

Example 13.11.2

Suggested elements to cover in a long abstract

1. Background (describe the problem area and its importance)
2. Research Hypotheses (or Research Purposes or Research Questions)
3. Method
4. Results
5. Implications
6. Suggestions for Further Research

The amount of emphasis to put on each element in an abstract is a subjective matter. When writing, keep in mind that the goal is to provide enough information for potential readers to make informed decisions on whether to read the entire research report.

➤ Guideline 13.12 Consider using subheadings in an abstract

Some journals require the use of subheadings, even in short abstracts. Subheadings may also be included in theses, dissertations, and term projects. Example 13.12.1 shows an abstract with subheadings (with the subheadings in bold for emphasis).

Example 13.12.1

Background. Mental health problems are a growing and significant issue in the Australian education system. Research has suggested that resilience can be learned and that schools can play an important role in developing resilient skills among youth; however, rigorous evaluation of interventions promoting resilience is limited. **Aims**. As martial arts training has been found to have psychological benefits such as increased confidence and self-esteem, this study investigated whether a 10-week martial arts training programme was an efficacious sports-based mental health intervention that promoted resilience in secondary school students. **Sample**. Two hundred and eighty-three secondary school students (age range 12–14 years) participated in the study. **Methods**. The study examined the effects of martial arts training on participants' resilience by delivering a 10-week martial arts-based intervention in secondary school settings. The intervention was evaluated using quantitative methodology and an experimental research design using a randomized controlled trial which measured participant responses at baseline, post-intervention, and follow-up. **Results**. The study found that the martial arts-based intervention had a significantly positive effect on developing students' resilience. This was especially apparent when the intervention and control group's mean resilience outcomes were compared. Resilience outcomes appeared to be stronger immediately following the intervention compared with 12-week follow-up. **Conclusions**. Given the prevalence of mental illness among Australian youth, the current study provides robust evidence that students' resilience can be improved using martial arts-based interventions delivered in school settings.[11]

Exercises for Chapter 13

Part A

1. According to this chapter, with what should an abstract begin if space is limited?

2. In light of this chapter, would you expect to find highlights of the research methodology described in an abstract?

3. Should highlights of the results be included in an abstract?

4. Is it desirable to point out unexpected results in an abstract?

5. If a study is strongly tied to a theory, should the theory be named in the abstract?

6. Are there any major deficiencies in the following abstract? Explain.

Abstract: Two hundred second-grade students were administered a battery of published cognitive tests that measured a variety of academic achievement variables. The students were drawn from three elementary schools in a large, urban school district. All were tested near the end of second grade. Graduate students administered the tests in three sessions because students might become fatigued by taking the entire battery in a single testing session. The three research hypotheses were confirmed. Implications for cognitive development and directions for future research are discussed.

Part B

Locate an abstract for a research report published in a journal that you believe illustrates a majority of the guidelines in this chapter.

Notes

1 Brown, Ku, & Englehardt (2023, p. 545).
2 Wakai, Nawa, Yamaoka, & Fujiwara (2023, p. 1).
3 Xia & Li (2022, p. 1).
4 Irvine III (2019, p. 203).
5 Bond, Vasil, Derges, & Nichols (2023, p. 425).
6 Cavanagh & King (2020, p. 287).
7 Felmlee, Julien, & Francisco (2023, p. 1).
8 Tanaka (2019, p. 266).
9 Beach, Brown, & Cukrowicz (2021, p. 1759).
10 Vinnervik (2022, p. 213).
11 Moore, Woodcock, & Dudley (2021, p. 1369).

Chapter 14

A Closer Look at Writing Reports of Qualitative or Mixed Methods Research

This chapter is not intended to be an exhaustive guide to writing a qualitative or mixed methods research report. Given the diversity of sample materials (e.g., archival documents, ethnography, qualitative content analysis, etc.) caution must be used when applying the guidelines outlined in this chapter to your discipline.

With certain obvious exceptions, such as some of the guidelines on reporting statistical results, the guidelines in the previous chapters should be considered when writing reports of qualitative or mixed methods research. This chapter presents guidelines that are specific to reporting qualitative or mixed methods research and may need to be adjusted depending on the student's discipline.

> ### ➤ Guideline 14.1 Consider using the term *qualitative* in the title of the report

Because the vast majority of research in the social and behavioral sciences continues to be quantitative, using the term qualitative in a title helps interested readers locate qualitative research. Examples 14.1.1 and 14.1.2 show how some researchers have used the term in titles.

Example 14.1.1

Investigating the Teaching Experiences of Psychology Graduate Students with Disabilities: A Qualitative Study[1]

Example 14.1.2

Teaching Awards in Higher Education: A Qualitative Study of Motivation and Outcomes[2]

 DOI: 10.4324/9781003230410-15

Notice that in both the above titles, the term qualitative was used in the subtitles instead of the main titles. This is appropriate because most readers searching for research reports are probably more interested in the variables studied (e.g., teaching awards) than in the methodological approach (e.g., a qualitative study).

➤ Guideline 14.2 Consider using the terms *qualitative* or *mixed methods* in the abstract of the report

If space does not permit mention of the qualitative or mixed methods nature of a study in its title, consider mentioning it in the abstract, as illustrated in Examples 14.2.1 and 14.2.2 (italics added for emphasis).

Example 14.2.1

This *qualitative case study* explores one college teacher's emotional trajectory during volunteer teaching in a constrained (e.g., educationally and economically underdeveloped) context. The study shows that the teacher's emotions were continually shaped by external and internal factors over an academic year. The volunteer teacher's self-agency gradually emerged as a vital internal factor in regulating his fluctuating emotions and demonstrating his positive emotions for teaching. Additionally, while the teacher's emotions were generally expressed in a positive manner, in-the-moment emotions were also expressed negatively to galvanise students' learning.[3]

Example 14.2.2

Mentoring is a critical element in the well-being, socialization, and professional identity development of graduate students. Yet in music education little is known about the graduate student mentoring experience from the mentors' perspective. Therefore, the purpose of this *mixed-methods study* was to examine music teacher educators' perspectives on and experiences with graduate student mentoring.[4]

Guidelines 14.1 and 14.2 are especially important when qualitative or mixed methods research has been conducted on a topic that has traditionally been approached quantitatively. The use of qualitative methodology on such a topic is a distinguishing characteristic of the research.

➤ Guideline 14.3 Consider discussing the choice of qualitative over quantitative methodology

A discussion of the choice of qualitative over quantitative methodology is usually placed in the introduction of a research report or in the section on methods. This guideline is especially recommended when writing research for an audience that is quantitatively oriented, such as readers of a journal that usually publishes quantitative research.

Example 14.3.1 illustrates this guideline.

Example 14.3.1

Traditional research in epidemiology conducts statistical analysis of health data to track patterns in public health. Informing these statistical efforts via qualitative descriptions of participant experiences before, during, and after an intervention will help understand the implementation of the intervention.[5]

➤ Guideline 14.4 Consider "revealing yourself" to the readers

While quantitative researchers are taught to be objective and distance themselves from their research participants to avoid influencing the outcome, qualitative and mixed methods researchers recognize the inherently subjective nature of research. In addition, most qualitative researchers use methods that involve direct interactions between researchers and their participants such as in-depth interviews, participant observation, and focus groups. Because of the interactive nature of much qualitative research, some researchers consider it appropriate to describe themselves when the descriptions may be relevant to what is being studied. An appropriate place to do this is in the Analysis subsection of the main section on methods (see the arrow in Example 11.1.1 in Chapter 11).

The researchers who wrote Example 14.4.1 "revealed themselves" in the report on a study of educational learning environments.

Example 14.4.1

The researchers were university faculty and graduate students and consisted of a White/Middle Eastern woman, a White woman from the local region, a Nigerian Black man, and a Costa Rican Latina woman. All researchers are actively opposed to big-data algorithms that convey and perpetuate historical

---

and current racism and sexism at large scales. The lead author and director of the research project is a former computer science and mathematics instructor whose perspective has influenced the design of the current program.[6]

> ## Guideline 14.5 Avoid calling a sample *purposive* if it is actually a sample of convenience

A *purposive sample* is one that a researcher believes to be especially well suited for obtaining meaningful data on a particular research problem. In other words, it consists of participants that a researcher deliberately selects because they have characteristics that make them especially worthy of attention.

When researchers use participants who are selected simply because they are convenient (such as students who happen to be enrolled in a professor's psychology course), the sample should be identified as one of convenience—not purposive—by using a phrase such as "a sample of convenience" or "accidental sample." This is illustrated in Example 14.5.1.

Example 14.5.1

First, students selected the schools based on the convenience sample method and not based on purposeful sampling.[7]

> ## Guideline 14.6 If a purposive sample was used, state the basis for selection of participants

In Example 14.6.1, the researchers purposefully selected cases at the extreme of a distribution.

Example 14.6.1

A purposive sample of 20 EPs involved in teaching was interviewed about the social and psychological impacts of involvement.[8]

> ## Guideline 14.7 Describe how participants were recruited

Whether a sample of convenience or a purposive sample was used, readers are likely to be interested in how the participants were recruited. This is especially true when studying potentially sensitive issues because poor recruitment procedures may lead to highly atypical samples. Example 14.7.1 shows a description of the recruitment of African American men. Note that the researchers used a variety of recruitment procedures in a variety of geographical locations, which would be expected to result in a diverse sample. Also, note that despite these efforts, the researchers still characterize the sample as being a convenience sample.

Example 14.7.1

The data for this project were collected from a convenience sample of men residing in the following metropolitan areas: Michigan, Georgia, Maryland, New York, and Virginia. Consistent with the principles of community-based research … knowledgeable African American community residents (including research assistants associated with this project) actively participated in the recruitment process. Recruiters for the present study distributed and collected survey materials. Participants were recruited through public announcements, e-mail, fliers, and word of mouth. Surveys were also distributed in local businesses, barbershops, and on the campus of historically African American and predominantly European American college campuses. The initial data collection resulted in a snowball effect. In other words, as men completed the survey, some volunteered to distribute surveys to other men, whereas others offered to encourage other men to participate in the study.[9]

➤ **Guideline 14.8 Provide demographic information**

Demographics (i.e., background variables) help readers "see" the participants. Even though qualitative and mixed methods researchers sometimes avoid statistics in the reporting of results, when describing the demographics of participants, statistics can be useful. This is illustrated in Example 14.8.1.

Example 14.8.1

As shown in Table 1, approximately half of study participants were male (51.4%); 50.5% were Non-Hispanic White, 11.3% Non-Hispanic Black, 23.8% Hispanic, 8.4% Asian, 1.2% Native Hawaiian, other Pacific Islander/American Indian, or Alaskan native, and 4.9% were classified as two or more races. 47.7% of households were below 200% of the federal poverty level. About 37.1% of parents had some schooling up to a high school degree/equivalent and approximately 78% of study participants lived in two parent households. 18.4% of participants spoke a non-English primary language in the home.[10]

> ## Guideline 14.9 Provide specific information on data collection methods

In an interview study, it is insufficient to state merely that "in-depth, semistructured interviews were conducted." Readers will want to know how the initial questions were developed as well as the topics these questions were designed to cover. Example 14.9.1 illustrates this.

Example 14.9.1

Data collection consisted of in-depth interviews conducted throughout the country, based on a semistructured interview guide. The interview guide for the larger study covered several content categories related to the experience of children and their perception of each stage of the escalation process, including their involvement in it. The part of the interview guide that related to the children's ongoing daily reality—their daily routine following the violence, on which this article is based—included questions such as the following: Can you tell me which people in your house talk to each other? What do you usually do together? Who talks to whom and about what? The interviews were conducted in two or three sessions of approximately 90 min each, depending on the pace set by the child. As special skills were required in interviewing children, each participant was individually interviewed by the author. The interviews were recorded and transcribed verbatim.[11]

Note that it may not be necessary to state the actual questions used, especially if the wording of the questions varied somewhat from participant to participant and the content of the questions changed over the course of a qualitative study in light of the data collected from earlier participants. On the other hand, if there were key questions that were asked of all participants, consider including them in the research report. If there were many questions, either provide just a sample for each domain of interest or provide them all in a table or appendix.

In Example 14.9.2, the researchers describe the areas covered by the questions and then refer the readers to a table that contains a list of open-ended questions (e.g., "What is your experience with regard to students and domestic violence, if any?"). Note that it may be desirable to identify (a) the individual(s) who conducted the interviews, (b) when and where the interviews were conducted, and (c) the basis for developing the interview guide.

Example 14.9.2

The interview schedule was created by the researchers and included questions regarding the experiences, school protocols, and support and training needs of school leaders and school staff in the area of DV [domestic violence]. To address the research questions, a list of open-ended questions was used during the interviews with school leaders (Table 2).[12]

Providing details on data collection is also desirable when reporting on observational studies. Consider answering questions such as these when writing the description: Was the observer a participant or nonparticipant? When were the observations made? Where were the observations made? How often were they made? How were the data recorded? For what types of behaviors did the researcher initially look? What types of changes took place in the data collection method as the collection of data proceeded?

➤ **Guideline 14.10 Describe steps taken to ensure the trustworthiness of the data**

Qualitative and mixed methods researchers use a variety of methods to ensure that their data are trustworthy. These should be described in enough detail to reassure readers that the data are not merely the reflection of one researcher's personal opinions. For instance, when "member checks" are used, describe how the activity was conducted and by whom, as illustrated in Example 14.10.1.

Example 14.10.1

Before proceeding with the analysis of the focus group data, the major themes identified by the researchers as well as the examples selected to support the themes were presented in writing to a sample of 10 of the 20 participants. Although all 20 were invited to participate in this phase of the research, only 10 were available at the appointed time for this activity. The first stage of the member check was to have the 10 participants highlight with a marker those themes and examples that they deemed most important. They were also asked to cross out any that seemed to be off track or unrepresentative of their understandings of the members' meanings in the focus groups. The second stage was to hold two small-group meetings with five participants each to discuss the material they highlighted and crossed out. This activity was conducted by …

Likewise, if "triangulation of data sources" was used to ensure trustworthiness, describe what each source was (e.g., parents, children, and teachers) and specifically how the data were collected from each source. Also, if "triangulation of methods of data collection" was used (e.g., interviews as well as observations), describe each clearly.

As a general rule, the methods used to ensure trustworthiness, including others not mentioned here, should not simply be mentioned in passing in a research report. Instead, they should be described in some detail.

➤ **Guideline 14.11 If two or more researchers participated in analyzing the data, describe how they arrived at a consensus**

In qualitative and mixed methods research, two or more individuals often participate in the analysis of the data. When this is done, readers will be interested in knowing about the extent to which these individuals were in agreement. Questions that might be addressed in light of this guideline are: Did the researchers analyze the data independently and then confer, or did they analyze it together from the beginning? If there were disagreements on some aspects of the interpretation, how were they resolved? How confident does each researcher feel in the final interpretations presented in the report?

➤ **Guideline 14.12 In the Results section of a qualitative report, provide quantitative results on quantitative matters**

Conducting qualitative or mixed methods research does not preclude the use of statistics in reports on the research because some matters naturally lend themselves to quantification. Note that the term "many" in Example 14.12.1 is a quantitative term because it clearly implies that some number of students had their heads down. Yet, the term "many" is unnecessarily vague if the researcher knows how many students or what percentage of students did this. The improved version is consistent with this guideline.

Example 14.12.1

Many of the students were observed to have their heads down on their desks during the mathematics lesson.

Improved Version of Example 14.12.1

About 25% of the students were observed to have their heads down on their desks during the mathematics lesson.

In short, just because the main analysis in a qualitative or mixed methods research project is nonquantitative does not rule out the use of statistics when they are appropriate.

➤ Guideline 14.13 Consider using the major themes as subheadings in the Results section

Often, the results of qualitative and mixed methods research are described in terms of major and minor themes. If the Results section of a report on qualitative or mixed methods research is long, consider using the names of the major themes as subheadings. This will help readers follow the organization of the results. In a report on adolescent thoughts and feelings about the environment, the authors of Example 14.13.1 used the themes and subthemes shown below.

Example 14.13.1

Major themes (**in bold**) and subthemes (*in italics*) used as subheadings in the Results section

Impact of the local environment
    Harmful influences
    Helpful influences
Efficacy
    Progress and empowerment
    Powerlessness
Challenging emotions
Information
    Responses
Hindrances
    Indifference
    Power/responsibility
    Other/competing priorities
Perceptions of the future
    Hopeful for change
    Catastrophic[13]

➣ Guideline 14.14 If quotations are reported, consider stating the basis for their selection

In qualitative and mixed methods research, large amounts of narrative material (the raw data) are often collected. Readers will be interested in learning the basis for the selection of the limited number of quotations presented in the Results section of a research report. Note that there may be different reasons for the selection of various quotations. Some might be selected because they are the most articulate expressions of a recurring theme. Others might be selected because they are the most emotional. The most common basis for selecting quotations is that they are *representative* of what a number of participants stated, which is illustrated in Example 14.14.1, in which the researchers indicate that the quotations illustrate a theme that was noted 21 times.

Example 14.14.1

This fear of HIV often extended to the fear of HIV testing. One participant explained that people in the community do not want to get tested because "they are scared that they will detect it [HIV]" (Female, Age 26, Mexico). Another participant elaborated: "They [Immigrants] are scared of getting the test because of fear of knowing that they're positive. It's better not to know. If they know, it can create a strong impact. Sometimes, I think we prefer to ignore these situations before looking at reality in hopes that they won't affect us" (Male, Age 45, Ecuador).

The notion of HIV as potential stress and trauma facilitated avoidance of testing and preventive health behaviors. Immigrants explained the competing priorities in their lives and noted that their own health was among their last concerns. "They [Immigrants] just don't care" (Female, Age 25, Dominican Republic) said one participant when asked about HIV in her community. Taken together, there was an overwhelming preference to avoid the potential trauma of HIV and to place attention on issues of seemingly greater importance.[14]

➣ Guideline 14.15 Consider discussing alternative interpretations of the data and why they were rejected

If there are obvious alternative interpretations, explicitly discuss the reasons for rejecting them in the Results section. For instance, a researcher might use quotations or talk about trends in the data that run counter to the alternatives, which would help explain why one interpretation was selected over another.

Concluding Comments

Writing effective reports of research is an art that can be mastered only with careful modeling of the writing of skilled professionals and practice. To move beyond this book and become a master of empirical research writing, the most important thing you can do is read numerous examples of the research written by others—with attention to detail, style, and mechanics. Skimming articles or, worse yet, reading only the abstracts is not sufficient. Instead, you should read research reports in their entirety while evaluating them by asking questions such as the following: What makes a report effective or ineffective? At what points did you get lost while reading a report? What else could the researcher have done to assist you in following his or her line of reasoning? In short, by becoming a critical consumer of research written by others, you will become a skilled writer of empirical research reports.

Exercises for Chapter 14

Part A

1. According to this chapter, is it more appropriate to put the term *qualitative* in a subtitle or to put it in the main title? Explain.

2. According to this chapter, when is it especially important to discuss the choice of qualitative methods over quantitative methods in a research report?

3. Because qualitative research often involves direct interactions between researchers and participants, what should researchers consider describing?

4. How is a *purposive sample* defined in this chapter?

5. When should researchers refer to their sample as a "sample of convenience"?

6. According to this chapter, is it ever appropriate to use statistics to present demographic information in a qualitative study?

7. According to this chapter, methods used to ensure trustworthiness should not be simply mentioned in passing in a research report. Instead, what should be done?

8. If two or more researchers participated in analyzing the data, what should be described in the research report?

9. Is it ever desirable to report quantities in the Results section of a report on qualitative research?

10. According to this chapter, what is the most common basis for selecting quotations from participants to include in a report on qualitative research?

11. Should alternative interpretations of the data be discussed in a qualitative research report?

Part B

Locate a report on qualitative research that you think illustrates many of the guidelines in this chapter.

Notes

1 Lund & Hanebutt (2022, p. 262).
2 Seppala & Smith (2020, p. 1398).
3 Zhang (2021, p. 203).
4 Bond, Vasil, Derges, & Nichols (2023, p. 425).
5 Pope, Cohen, & Duarte (2019, p. 6).
6 Irgens, Adisa, Bailey, & Quesada (2022, pp. 128–129).
7 Tabatadze & Chachkhiani (2021, p. 84).
8 Ward, Stanyon, Ryan, & Dave (2022, p. 549).
9 Hammond & Mattis (2005, p. 117).
10 Mann, Silver, & Stein (2021, p. 610).
11 Carmel (2019, p. 478).
12 Berger, Chionh, & Miko (2022, p. 1091).
13 Thompson et al. (2022, pp. 6–8).
14 Lee (2019, pp. 848–849).

Chapter 15

Preparing Reference Lists*

The reference list is usually the last element in a research report.[1] Researchers will cite journal articles in their research reports because journal articles are the major source of primary (i.e., original) reports of the research of others. Thus, this chapter emphasizes the preparation of a reference list that refers to journal articles. For details on referencing other types of sources, consult a style manual or the reference tools within online search databases (see Guideline 15.2).

It should be noted that a reference list is different from a bibliography. A reference list should contain references only to literature cited in the report (see Guideline 1.7).

➢ Guideline 15.1 "References" is a main heading that follows the main heading "Discussion"

Example 15.1.1 shows the placement of the reference list relative to the other parts of a research report discussed up to this point in this book (see the arrow in the Example).

Example 15.1.1

Title in Upper- and Lowercase Letters
Abstract (a main heading; centered in bold)
A literature review that introduces the research problem (with no heading)
Method (a main heading; centered in bold)
Participants (a subheading; flush left in bold)
Measures (a subheading; flush left in bold)

---

* Portions of this chapter were adapted with permission from Galvan & Galvan (2017). It is recommended that you consult their text for a more detailed explanation.

 DOI: 10.4324/9781003230410-16

Procedure (optional; a subheading; flush left in bold)
Analysis (optional; a subheading; flush left in bold)
   Results (a main heading; centered in bold)
  Discussion (a main heading; centered in bold)
  ⇨ **References** (a main heading; centered in bold)

➤ **Guideline 15.2 Select a style manual and carefully follow its directions for preparing a reference list**

A style manual specifies mechanical features such as spacing, margins, and levels of heading, as well as the preparation of reference lists for manuscripts written for a particular audience/discipline. For instance, the *Publication Manual of the American Psychological Association* prescribes mechanics for the preparation of manuscripts for publication in the journals published by the Association. Because of its comprehensive nature, it is also the style manual for many journals in other fields such as education, sociology, nursing, and kinesiology. Students may choose to consult the appropriate style manual online or directly export citations in the appropriate format while consulting online articles.

Example 15.2.1 shows a reference list entry for a journal article formatted in American Psychological Association (APA) style. Notice that many of the details of the style cannot be derived from intuition. For instance, the first and middle names of authors are not spelled out and the "&" sign, not the word *and*, is used when there are multiple authors. Also, APA style does not use the abbreviation "pp." before the page numbers in a reference list (e.g., 336–352 in Example 15.2.1 is *not* preceded with "pp.").

Example 15.2.1

McManus, D., Dryer, R., & Henning, M. (2017). Barriers to learning online experienced by students with a mental health disability. *Distance Education, 38*, 336–352.

Notice the use of a *hanging indent* (i.e., the first line is not indented but the subsequent lines in the reference are indented) in Example 15.2.1. The hanging indent makes the authors' names stand out in a reference list (examine the reference list for this book after this chapter).[2]

➤ **Guideline 15.3 A journal title is treated like a book title—italicize it**

Academic libraries used to collect all the issues of a journal for a year and have them case bound (i.e., put into a hardback cover). This would result in a "book" for each year of the journal. Thus, as with any other book, underline or italicize the titles of journals.

➤ **Guideline 15.4 Double-check punctuation in accordance with the style manual**

A style manual specifies the punctuation to be used in a reference list. For instance, if a style manual shows a period at the close of the parentheses containing the year of publication, be careful not to substitute a comma.

➤ **Guideline 15.5 Double-check capitalization in accordance with the style manual**

In APA style, for instance, only the first letter of the first word in the main title and in the subtitle of the journal article is capitalized. Capitalizing the letters of all major words in the title in a reference list is not APA style.[3]

➤ **Guideline 15.6 A reference list should only contain entries for works that have been cited in the research report**

Do not treat the reference list as a suggested reading list. Include only references for literature that was cited in the body of the research report.

➤ **Guideline 15.7 Cross-check reference citations in the body of the report with those in the reference list**

Examine each citation in the body of the research report and check to see that (a) it is included in the reference list, (b) names are spelled correctly in both places, and (c) years of publication are the same.

Concluding Comments

Preparing a reference list should be done with great care. Inaccurate or improperly formatted references can cost points when term-project reports are graded. In addition, carelessness could call into question the care with which other parts of a report were prepared.

Exercises for Chapter 15

1. What is missing from the following reference?

    Jones, B. F., & Smith, A. D. (2023). The relationship between job satisfaction and income level. *Journal of Labor*, 14–20.

2. What is missing from the following reference?

    Jones, B. F., Smith, A. D. (2023). The relationship between job satisfaction and income level. *Journal of Labor*, *35*, 14–20.

3. Are italics used appropriately in the following reference? Explain.

    Jones, B. F., & Smith, A. D. (2023). *The relationship between job satisfaction and income level.* Journal of Labor, *35*, 14–20.

4. What should be deleted from the following reference?

    Jones, B. F., & Smith, A. D. (2023). The relationship between job satisfaction and income level. *Journal of Labor*, *35*, pp. 14–20.

5. What should be changed in the following reference?

    Jones, Bernard F., & Smith, Amy D. (2023). The relationship between job satisfaction and income level. *Journal of Labor*, *35*, 14–20.

6. What is wrong with the punctuation in the following reference?

    Jones, B. F., & Smith, A. D. (2023), The relationship between job satisfaction and income level. *Journal of Labor*, *35*, 14–20.

7. What is wrong with the capitalization in the following reference?

    Jones, B. F., & Smith, A. D. (2023). The Relationship Between Job Satisfaction and Income Level. *Journal of Labor*, *35*, 14–20.

Notes

1   If there are appendices to a research report, these should be included after the reference list.
2   In Word, a hanging indent can be easily created by clicking on "Format," then "Paragraph," which will default to the "Indents and Spacing" dialog box. To reveal the word "Hanging," click on the down arrow under the word "Special." Then click on the word "Hanging" to create a hanging indent.
3   Also, proper names should be capitalized. This guideline *only* applies to the reference list. The first letters of all major words in the title of a research report (i.e., the title that appears at the beginning of the report) should be capitalized.

References

Adewumi, B., Bailey, L. R., Mires-Richards, E., Quinlan, K. M., Agyeman, E., Alabi, A., Jeyasingh, M., Konadu-Mensah, C., Lavinière, W., Mighton, P., Shortridge, T., Thomas, D. S. P., & Wassamba-Wabelua, N. (2022). Cross-disciplinary, collaborative and student-led: Developing a change process for diversifying reading lists. *London Review of Education, 20*(1), 1–17.

Almond, L., Parson, L., & Resor, J. (2021). Lessons from the field: Graduate student–faculty mentoring in family science. *Family Relations, 70*(5), 1600–1611.

Austin, M. R., Fogler, K. A. J., & Daniel, D. B. (2022). Seeing self and others on-screen does not negatively impact learning in virtual classrooms. *Scholarship of Teaching and Learning in Psychology, 8*(4), 368–373.

Beach, V. L., Brown, S. L., & Cukrowicz, K. C. (2021). Examining the relations between hopelessness, thwarted interpersonal needs, and passive suicide ideation among older adults: Does meaning in life matter? *Aging & Mental Health, 25*(9), 1759–1767.

Beasley, C. R., & Xiao, Y. J. (2023). Incarceration history and ethnic bias in hiring perceptions: An experimental test of intersectional bias and psychological mechanisms. *PLoS ONE, 17*(1), 1–13.

Berger, E., Chionh, N., & Miko, A. (2022). School leaders' experiences on dealing with students exposed to domestic violence. *Journal of Family Violence, 37*(7), 1089–1100.

Bond, V. L., Vasil, M., Derges, J. D., & Nichols, B. E. (2023). Mentoring graduate students in music education: A mixed-methods phenomenological study. *Journal of Research in Music Education, 70*(4), 425–448.

Borelli, J. L., Cervantes, B. R., Hecht, H. K., Marquez, C. M., DePrado, R., Torres, G., Robles, A., Chirinos, N., Leal, F., Montiel, G. I., Pedroza, M., & Guerra, N. (2022). Barreras y soluciones: Lessons learned from integrating research-based clinical techniques into a community agency serving low-income Latinx immigrant families. *Family Process, 61*(1), 108–129.

Borsotti, M., Mosca, I. E., Di Lauro, F., Pancani, S., Bracali, C., Dore, T., Macchi, C., Cecchi, F., & IRCCS Don Gnocchi Stroke Group. (2020). The visual scanning test: A newly developed neuropsychological tool to assess and target rehabilitation of extrapersonal visual unilateral spatial neglect. *Neurological Sciences, 41*(5), 1145–1152.

Brown, C. P., Ku, D. H., & Englehardt, J. (2023). Mixed understandings: A case study of how a sample of preschool stakeholders made sense of the Changed Kindergarten. *Early Childhood Education Journal, 51*(3), 545–557.

Bushman, B. B., & Peacock, G. G. (2010). Does teaching problem-solving skills matter? An evaluation of problem-solving skills training for the treatment of social and behavioral problems in children. *Child & Family Behavior Therapy, 32*, 103–124.

Carmel, Y. (2019). The experience of "nothingness" among children exposed to interparental violence. *Journal of Loss & Trauma, 24*(5/6), 473–494.

Cavanagh, M., & King, A. (2020). Peer-group mentoring for primary pre-service teachers during professional experience. *Asia-Pacific Journal of Teacher Education, 48*(3), 287–300.

Chan, M., Sharkey, J. D., Lawrie, S. I., Arch, D. A. N., & Nylund-Gibson, K. (2021). Elementary school teacher well-being and supportive measures amid COVID-19: An exploratory study. *School Psychology, 36*(6), 533–545.

Chung, D., Chen, Y., & Meng, Y. (2023). Perceived information overload and intention to discontinue use of short-form video: The mediating roles of cognitive and psychological factors. *Behavioral Sciences, 13*(1), 1–15.

Clarke, B., Turtura, J., Lesner, T., Cook, M., Smolkowski, K., Kosty, D., & Doabler, C. T. (2022). A conceptual replication of a kindergarten math intervention within the context of a research-based core. *Exceptional Children, 89*(1), 42–59.

Coates, M., & Macfadyen, A. (2021). Student experiences of a return to practice programme: A qualitative study. *British Journal of Nursing, 30*(15), 900–908.

Crawford, L. A., & Novak, K. B. (2020). College student activities, social capital, and drinking behavior. *Journal of Alcohol & Drug Education, 64*(1), 8–32.

Da Rocha Rodrigues, G., Anex, A., Boegli, M., Bollondi Pauly, C., Curtin, F., Luthy, C., Desmeules, J., & Cedraschi, C. (2023). Is massage a legitimate part of nursing care? A qualitative study. *PLoS ONE, 17*(2), 1–15.

Dashti, F. A., & Habeeb, K. M. (2020). Impact of shared iPads on kindergarten students' collaboration and engagement in visual storytelling activities. *Early Childhood Education Journal, 48*(4), 521–531.

Dohnt, H., & Tiggemann, M. (2006). The contribution of peer and media influences to the development of body satisfaction and self-esteem in young girls: A prospective study. *Developmental Psychology, 42*, 929–936.

Douglas, S. N., Meadan, H., & Schultheiss, H. (2022). A meta-synthesis of caregivers' experiences transitioning from early intervention to early childhood special education. *Early Childhood Education Journal, 50*(3), 371–383.

Downes, N., Lichtlé, J., Lamore, K., Orêve, M.-J., & Cappe, E. (2021). Couples' experiences of parenting a child after an autism diagnosis: A qualitative study. *Journal of Autism & Developmental Disorders, 51*(8), 2697–2710.

Felmlee, D. H., Julien, C., & Francisco, S. C. (2023). Debating stereotypes: Online reactions to the vice-presidential debate of 2020. *PLoS ONE, 17*(1), 1–22.

Freeman-Wong, R. E., Mazumder, T., & Cisneros, J. (2022). Keep fighting for existence: Undocumented student resource centers as counter-spaces within community colleges. *Community College Review, 50*(4), 436–455.

Galvan, J. L., & Galvan, M. C. (2017). *Writing literature reviews: A guide for students of the social and behavioral sciences* (7th ed.). London: Routledge.

Haddad, J. M., Macenski, C., Mosier-Mills, A., Hibara, A., Kester, K., Schneider, M., Conrad, R. C., & Liu, C. H. (2021). The impact of social media on college mental health during the COVID-19 pandemic: A multinational review of the existing literature. *Current Psychiatry Reports, 23*(11), 1–12.

Hammond, W. P., & Mattis, J. S. (2005). Being a man about it: Manhood meaning among African American men. *Psychology of Men & Masculinity, 6*, 114–126.

Heintzman, J., Hwang, J., Quiñones, A. R., Guzman, C. E. V., Bailey, S. R., Lucas, J., Giebultowicz, S., Chan, B., & Marino, M. (2022). Influenza and pneumococcal vaccination delivery in older Hispanic populations in the United States. *Journal of the American Geriatrics Society, 70*(3), 854–861.

Hewitt, P. L., Kealy, D., Mikail, S. F., Smith, M. M., Ge, S., Chen, C., Sochting, I., Tasca, G. A., Flett, G. L., & Ko, A. (2023). The efficacy of group psychotherapy for adults with perfectionism: A randomized controlled trial of dynamic-relational therapy versus psychodynamic supportive therapy. *Journal of Consulting and Clinical Psychology, 91*(1), 29–42.

Holland, M. M. (2020). Framing the search: How first-generation students evaluate colleges. *Journal of Higher Education, 91*(3), 378–401.

Irgens, G. A., Adisa, I., Bailey, C., & Quesada, H. V. (2022). Designing with and for youth: A participatory design research approach for critical machine learning education. *Journal of Educational Technology & Society, 25*(4), 126–141.

Irvine III, F. R. (2019). Academic success of African American males in a historically black university. *Journal of African American Studies, 23*(3), 203–216.

Jowsey, T., Petersen, L., Mysko, C., Cooper-Ioelu, P., Herbst, P., Webster, C. S., Wearn, A., Marshall, D., Torrie, J., Lin, M.-J. P., Beaver, P., Egan, J., Bacal, K., O'Callaghan, A., & Weller, J. (2020). Performativity, identity formation and professionalism: Ethnographic research to explore student experiences of clinical simulation training. *PLoS ONE, 15*(7), 1–16.

Joyce, A., & Hassenfeldt, T. A. (2020). Utility of a peer teaching mentor to graduate teaching assistants. *College Teaching, 68*(1), 12–19.

Kadur, J., Huber, D., Klug, G., Müller, S., Wendt, L., & Andreas, S. (2022). Passing patients' tests—But how? An analysis of therapists' helping skills in response to patient testing. *Journal of Counseling Psychology, 69*(6), 845–852.

Lassander, M., Hintsanen, M., Ravaja, N., Määttänen, I., Suominen, S., Mullola, S., Makkonen, T., Vahlberg, T., & Volanen, S.-M. (2022). Pilot study on students' stress reactivity after mindfulness intervention compared to relaxation control group. *International Journal of Stress Management, 29*(3), 306–317.

Lee, A. N., Muller, S., & McDermott, K. (2021). Under pressure: Tailored CPR with stress management for formerly incarcerated individuals. *COABE Journal, 10*(1), 4–22.

Lee, E.-J., Ditchman, N., Thomas, J., & Tsen, J. (2019). Microaggressions experienced by people with multiple sclerosis in the workplace: An exploratory study using Sue's taxonomy. *Rehabilitation Psychology, 64*(2), 179–193.

Lee, J. J. (2019). Cumulative stress and trauma from the migration process as barriers to HIV testing: A qualitative study of Latino immigrants. *Journal of Immigrant & Minority Health, 21*(4), 844–852.

Lund, E. M., & Hanebutt, R. A. (2022). Investigating the teaching experiences of psychology graduate students with disabilities: A qualitative study. *Rehabilitation Psychology, 67*(3), 262–272.

Main, J. B., Johnson, B. N., & Wang, Y. (2021). Gatekeepers of engineering workforce diversity? The academic and employment returns to student participation in voluntary cooperative education programs. *Research in Higher Education, 62*(4), 448–477.

Mann, M., Silver, E. J., & Stein, R. E. K. (2021). Kindergarten children's academic skills: Association with public library use, shared book reading and poverty. *Reading Psychology*, *42*(6), 606–624.

Martinez, M. A., Vega, D., & Marquez, J. (2019). Latinx students' experiences with college access and preparation at college preparatory charter schools. *Journal of Latinos & Education*, *18*(1), 28–41.

McGarity-Shipley, E. C., Jadidi, N., & Pyke, K. E. (2022). A pilot study assessing effectiveness of a written shame induction protocol with and without a social evaluative threat manipulation. *Canadian Journal of Behavioural Science/Revue Canadienne des Sciences du Comportement*, *54*(4), 257–267.

McManus, D., Dryer, R., & Henning, M. (2017). Barriers to learning online experienced by students with a mental health disability. *Distance Education*, *38*(3), 336–352.

Mikaelsson, K., Rutberg, S., Lindqvist, A.-K., & Michaelson, P. (2020). Physically inactive adolescents' experiences of engaging in physical activity. *European Journal of Physiotherapy*, *22*(4), 191–196.

Moore, B., Woodcock, S., & Dudley, D. (2021). Well-being warriors: A randomized controlled trial examining the effects of martial arts training on secondary students' resilience. *British Journal of Educational Psychology*, *91*(4), 1369–1394.

Mullikin, K., Stransky, M., Tendulkar, S., Casey, M., & Kosinski, K. (2021). Informal preparation and years of experience: Key correlates of dyslexia knowledge among Massachusetts early elementary teachers. *Dyslexia*, *27*(4), 510–524.

Nicola, T. P. (2022). Assessing applicants in context? School profiles and their implications for equity in the selective college admission process. *Journal of Diversity in Higher Education*, *15*(6), 700–715.

Parish, T., Baghurst, T., & Turner, R. (2010). Becoming competitive amateur bodybuilders: Identification of contributors. *Psychology of Men & Masculinity*, *11*, 152–159.

Peterson, S. M., Eldridge, R. R., Rios, D., & Schenk, Y. A. (2019). Ethical challenges encountered in delivering behavior analytic services through teleconsultation. *Behavior Analysis: Research and Practice*, *19*(2), 190–201.

Pinto, R. M., Kay, E. S., Choi, C. J., & Wall, M. M. (2020). Interprofessional collaboration improves linkages to primary care: A longitudinal analysis. *AIDS Care*, *32*(8), 970–978.

Pitimson, N. (2021). Teaching death to undergraduates: Exploring the student experience of discussing emotive topics in the university classroom. *Educational Review*, *73*(4), 470–486.

Pope, A., Cohen, A. K., & Duarte, C. D. P. (2019). Making civic engagement go viral: Applying social epidemiology principles to civic education. *Journal of Public Affairs*, *19*(1), 1–10.

Rancourt, D., Ahlich, E., Choquette, E. M., Simon, J., & Kelley, K. (2022). A comparison of food and alcohol disturbance (FAD) in sorority and non-sorority women. *Journal of American College Health*, *70*(1), 30–33.

Ren, L., Chen, J., Li, X., Wu, H., Fan, J., & Li, L. (2021). Extracurricular activities and Chinese children's school readiness: Who benefits more? *Child Development*, *92*(3), 1028–1047.

Ritter, C., Morrison, J. Q., & Sherman, K. (2021). Differential effects of self-graphing on self-monitoring of early literacy outcomes in kindergarten students. *Journal of Behavioral Education*, *30*(4), 559–577.

Robinson, A. (1988). Thinking straight and writing that way: Publishing in the *Gifted Child Quarterly*. *Gifted Child Quarterly, 32*(4), 367–369.

Schoppe-Sullivan, S. J., Shafer, K., Olofson, E. L., & Kamp Dush, C. M. (2021). Fathers' parenting and coparenting behavior in dual-earner families: Contributions of traditional masculinity, father nurturing role beliefs, and maternal gate closing. *Psychology of Men & Masculinities, 22*(3), 538–550.

Scott, L. D., Hofmeister, N., Rogness, N., & Rogers, A. E. (2010). An interventional approach for patient and nurse safety: A fatigue countermeasures feasibility study. *Nursing Research, 59*, 250–258.

Seppala, N., & Smith, C. (2020). Teaching awards in higher education: A qualitative study of motivation and outcomes. *Studies in Higher Education, 45*(7), 1398–1412.

Simm, I., Winklhofer, U., Naab, T., Langmeyer, A. N., & Linberg, A. (2021). How children and adolescents perceive their coping with home learning in times of COVID-19: A mixed method approach. *Frontiers in Psychology, 12*, 1–17.

Simmons-Horton, S. Y. (2021). "A bad combination": Lived experiences of youth involved in the foster care and juvenile justice systems. *Child & Adolescent Social Work Journal, 38*(6), 583–597.

Sipan, C. L., Portillo-Silva, C., Bang, H., & McCurdy, S. (2022). Coccidioidomycosis knowledge and behaviors of California Hispanic farm workers. *Journal of Agromedicine, 27*(2), 197–206.

Stotzer, R., Godinet, M. T., & Davidson, J. T. (2020). Unique characteristics of bias crimes committed by males or females in the United States. *Journal of Hate Studies, 16*(1), 35–46.

Tabatadze, S., & Chachkhiani, K. (2021). COVID-19 and emergency remote teaching in the country of Georgia: Catalyst for educational change and reforms in Georgia? *Educational Studies, 57*(1), 78–95.

Tanaka, T. (2019). Using mental imagery to manipulate the future time perspective of young adults: Effects on attentional bias in relation to depressive tendencies. *Journal of Adult Development, 26*(4), 266–274.

Theobald, R. J., Goldhaber, D. D., Holden, K. L., & Stein, M. L. (2022). Special education teacher preparation, literacy instructional alignment, and reading achievement for students with high-incidence disabilities. *Exceptional Children, 88*(4), 381–400.

Thompson, R., Fisher, H. L., Dewa, L. H., Hussain, T., Kabba, Z., & Toledano, M. B. (2022). Adolescents' thoughts and feelings about the local and global environment: A qualitative interview study. *Child & Adolescent Mental Health, 27*(1), 4–13.

Tomić, I., Pinćjer, I., Dedijer, S., & Adamović, S. (2022). Online learning during COVID-19 pandemic as perceived by the students of graphic engineering and design. *Journal of Graphic Engineering & Design, 13*(2), 15–20.

Tsai, C.-L., Ku, H.-Y., & Campbell, A. (2021). Impacts of course activities on student perceptions of engagement and learning online. *Distance Education, 42*(1), 106–125.

Tsang, K. K. Y., Shum, K. K., Chan, W. W. L., Li, S. X., Kwan, H. W., Su, M. R., Wong, B. P. H., & Lam, S. F. (2021). Effectiveness and mechanisms of mindfulness training for school teachers in difficult times: A randomized controlled trial. *Mindfulness, 12*(11), 2820–2831.

Vincent, J., & Ralston, K. (2020). Trainee teachers' knowledge of autism: Implications for understanding and inclusive practice. *Oxford Review of Education, 46*(2), 202–221.

Vinnervik, P. (2022). Implementing programming in school mathematics and technology: Teachers' intrinsic and extrinsic challenges. *International Journal of Technology & Design Education, 32*(1), 213–242.

Wakai, H., Nawa, N., Yamaoka, Y., & Fujiwara, T. (2023). Stressors and coping strategies among single mothers during the COVID-19 pandemic. *PLoS ONE, 17*(3), 1–13.

Ward, K., Stanyon, M., Ryan, K., & Dave, S. (2022). Power, recovery and doing something worthwhile: A thematic analysis of expert patient perspectives in psychiatry education. *Health Expectations, 25*(2), 549–557.

Wei, Y., Carr, W., Alaffe, R., & Kutcher, S. (2020). Mental health literacy development: Application of online and in-person professional development for preservice teachers to address knowledge, stigma, and help-seeking intentions. *Canadian Journal of Behavioural Science/Revue Canadienne des Sciences du Comportement, 52*(2), 107–114.

Will, P., Bischof, W. F., & Kingstone, A. (2020). The impact of classroom seating location and computer use on student academic performance. *PLoS ONE, 15*(8), 1–11.

Xia, T., & Li, Z. (2022). Behavioral training of high-functioning autistic children by music education of occupational therapy. *Occupational Therapy International, 2022,* 1–10.

Xin, J. F., & Affrunti, L. R. (2019). Using iPads in vocabulary instruction for English language learners. *Computers in the Schools, 36*(1), 69–82.

Zhang, J., & Gonzales-Backen, M. A. (2023). The association between acculturative stress and rule-breaking behaviors among Latinx adolescents in rural areas: A moderated mediation analysis. *Cultural Diversity and Ethnic Minority Psychology,* 1–10. https://psycnet.apa.org/record/2023-52912-001

Zhang, X. (2021). Understanding teachers' emotional trajectory: The voice of a volunteer teacher in an educationally and economically underdeveloped context. *Asia-Pacific Journal of Teacher Education, 49*(2), 203–215.

Zsila, Á., Orosz, G., McCutcheon, L. E., & Demetrovics, Z. (2021). Investigating the association between celebrity worship and heteronormative attitudes among heterosexual and LGB+ individuals. *Sexuality & Culture, 25*(4), 1334–1352.

A Checklist of Guidelines

Instructors may wish to refer to the following checklist numbers when commenting on students' papers (e.g., "See Guideline 5.2"). Students can also use this checklist to review important points as they prepare their research reports and proposals.

Chapter 1 Structuring a Research Report

☐ 1.1 A research report typically has a brief title.

☐ 1.2 An abstract usually follows the title.

☐ 1.3 The body of a typical research report begins with a literature review, which serves as the introduction to the research project.

☐ 1.4 The Method section describes the participants, the measures, and other details on how the research was conducted.

☐ 1.5 The Results section presents the findings.

☐ 1.6 The Discussion section presents the researcher's interpretations.

☐ 1.7 The reference list should contain references only to literature cited in the report.

☐ 1.8 In long reports, use additional second- and third-level headings.

Chapter 2 Writing Simple Research Hypotheses

☐ 2.1 A simple research hypothesis should name two variables and indicate the type of relationship expected between them.

☐ 2.2 When there is an independent variable, name a specific dependent variable.

☐ 2.3 Consider naming population(s) in the hypothesis.

☐ 2.4 A simple hypothesis should usually be expressed in a single sentence.

☐ 2.5 Even a simple hypothesis should be as specific as possible within a single sentence.

☐ 2.6 If a comparison is to be made, the elements to be compared should be stated.

☐ 2.7 Because most hypotheses deal with the behavior of groups, plural forms should usually be used.

☐ 2.8 Avoid gender stereotypes in the statement of a hypothesis.

☐ 2.9 A hypothesis should be free of terms and phrases that do not add to its meaning.

☐ 2.10 A hypothesis should indicate what will be studied—not the possible implications of a study or value judgments of the author.

☐ 2.11 A hypothesis should name variables in the order in which they occur or will be measured.

☐ 2.12 Avoid using the words *significant* or *significance* in a hypothesis.

☐ 2.13 Avoid using the word *prove* in a hypothesis.

☐ 2.14 Avoid using two different terms to refer to the same variable in a hypothesis.

☐ 2.15 Avoid making precise statistical predictions in a hypothesis.

Chapter 3 A Closer Look at Hypotheses

☐ 3.1 A single sentence may contain more than one hypothesis.

☐ 3.2 When a number of related hypotheses are to be stated, consider presenting them in a numbered or lettered list.

☐ 3.3 The hypothesis or hypotheses should be stated before the Method section.

☐ 3.4 While some researchers use alternative terms, the term *hypothesis* is preferred.

☐ 3.5 In a research report, a hypothesis should flow from the narrative that immediately precedes it.

☐ 3.6 Both directional and nondirectional hypotheses are acceptable.

☐ 3.7 When a researcher has a research hypothesis, it should be stated; the null hypothesis need not always be stated.

Chapter 4 Writing Research Objectives and Questions

☐ 4.1 When no relationship will be examined, consider stating a research objective.

☐ 4.2 When no relationship will be examined, consider posing a research question.

☐ 4.3 Stating a research objective or posing a research question are equally acceptable.

☐ 4.4 Avoid writing a research question that implies that the answer will be a simple "yes" or "no."

☐ 4.5 When previous research is contradictory, consider using a research objective or a research question instead of a hypothesis.

☐ 4.6 When a new topic is to be examined, consider using a research objective or a research question instead of a hypothesis.

☐ 4.7 For *qualitative* research, consider writing a research objective or question instead of a hypothesis.

☐ 4.8 A research objective or question should be as specific as possible yet be comprehensible.

☐ 4.9 When stating related objectives or questions, consider presenting them in a numbered or lettered list.

☐ 4.10 A research objective or question should flow from the literature review that immediately precedes it.

Chapter 5 Writing Titles

☐ 5.1 If only a small number of variables are studied, the title should name the variables.

☐ 5.2 A title should not be a complete sentence.

☐ 5.3 If many variables are studied, only the types of variables should be named.

☐ 5.4 The title of a journal article should be concise; the title of a thesis or dissertation may be longer.

☐ 5.5 A title should indicate what was studied—not the findings of the study.

☐ 5.6 Consider mentioning the population(s) in a title.

☐ 5.7 Consider the use of subtitles to indicate the methods of study.

☐ 5.8 If a study is strongly tied to a particular model or theory, consider mentioning it in the title.

☐ 5.9 Omit the names of specific measures unless they are the focus of the research.

☐ 5.10 A title may be in the form of a question, but this form should be used sparingly and with caution.

☐ 5.11 In titles, use the words *effect* and *influence* with caution.

☐ 5.12 A title should be consistent with the research hypothesis, objective, purpose, or question.

☐ 5.13 Consider mentioning unique features of a study in its title.

☐ 5.14 Avoid using "clever" titles.

☐ 5.15 Learn the conventions for capitalization in titles.

Chapter 6 Writing Introductions and Literature Reviews

☐ 6.1 In theses and dissertations, the first chapter is usually an introduction.

☐ 6.2 In theses and dissertations, the second chapter presents a comprehensive literature review.

☐ 6.3 In most research reports, literature reviews serve as the introduction to the reports.

☐ 6.4 In most research reports, literature reviews are selective.

☐ 6.5 A literature review should be an essay—not a list of annotations.

☐ 6.6 A literature review should lead logically to research hypotheses, objectives, or questions.

☐ 6.7 Research hypotheses, objectives, or questions should usually be stated at the end of the literature review.

☐ 6.8 Research reports with similar findings or methodologies should usually be cited together.

☐ 6.9 The importance of a topic should be explicitly stated.

☐ 6.10 Consider pointing out the number or percentage of individuals who are affected by the problem.

☐ 6.11 Discuss theories that have relevance to the current research.

☐ 6.12 Consider commenting on the relevance and importance of the research being cited.

☐ 6.13 Point out trends in the literature.

☐ 6.14 Point out gaps in the literature.

☐ 6.15 Be prepared to justify statements regarding gaps in the literature.

☐ 6.16 Point out how the current study differs from previous studies.

☐ 6.17 Use direct quotations sparingly.

☐ 6.18 Report sparingly on the details of the literature being cited.

☐ 6.19 Consider using literature to provide the historical context for the present study.

☐ 6.20 Consider citing prior literature reviews.

☐ 6.21 When using the "author-date method" for citing references, decide whether to emphasize authorship or content.

☐ 6.22 Avoid referring to the credentials and affiliations of the researchers.

☐ 6.23 Terminology in a literature review should reflect the tentative nature of empirical data.

☐ 6.24 Avoid using long strings of reference citations for a single finding or theory.

☐ 6.25 Use of the first person is acceptable if used sparingly.

☐ 6.26 In long literature reviews, start with a paragraph that describes its organization and use subheadings.

☐ 6.27 Consider ending long and complex literature reviews with a brief summary.

Chapter 7 Writing Definitions

☐ 7.1 All variables in a research hypothesis, objective, or question should be defined.

☐ 7.2 The defining attributes of a population (also called *control variables*) should be defined.

☐ 7.3 Key concepts in theories on which the research is based should be defined.

☐ 7.4 A conceptual definition should be sufficiently specific to differentiate it from related concepts.

☐ 7.5 Consider quoting published conceptual definitions.

☐ 7.6 Consider providing examples to amplify conceptual definitions.

☐ 7.7 Operational definitions usually should be provided in the Method section of a report.

☐ 7.8 Consider providing operational definitions for each conceptual definition.

☐ 7.9 If a published measure was used, the variable measured by it may be operationally defined by citing reference(s).

☐ 7.10 If an unpublished measure was used, consider reproducing sample questions or the entire measure.

☐ 7.11 Operational definitions should be specific enough so that another researcher can replicate the study.

☐ 7.12 Even a highly operational definition may not be a useful definition.

Chapter 8 Writing Assumptions, Limitations, and Delimitations

☐ 8.1 When stating an assumption, consider providing the reason(s) why it was necessary to make the assumption.

☐ 8.2 If there is a reason for believing that an assumption is true, state the reason.

☐ 8.3 If an assumption is highly questionable, consider casting it as a limitation.

☐ 8.4 Distinguish between limitations and delimitations.

☐ 8.5 Discuss limitations and delimitations separately.

☐ 8.6 Consider elaborating on the nature of a limitation.

☐ 8.7 Consider speculating on the possible effects of a limitation on the results of a study.

☐ 8.8 If a study has serious limitations, consider labeling it a pilot study.

☐ 8.9 Consider pointing out strengths as well as limitations.

Chapter 9 Writing Method Sections

☐ 9.1 Provide a brief overview of the method used.

☐ 9.2 Describe the sample.

☐ 9.3 If applicable, decide whether to use the term *participants* or *subjects* to refer to the individuals studied.

☐ 9.4 Describe the informed consent procedures, if any.

☐ 9.5 Consider describing steps taken to maintain confidentiality of the data.

☐ 9.6 The participants should be described in enough detail for the reader to visualize them.

☐ 9.7 Consider reporting demographics in tables.

☐ 9.8 When a sample is very small, consider providing a description of individual participants.

☐ 9.9 If only a sample was studied, the method of sampling should be described.

☐ 9.10 Explicitly acknowledge weaknesses in sampling.

☐ 9.11 Provide detailed information on nonparticipants when possible.

☐ 9.12 Describe the measures after describing the participants.

☐ 9.13 Describe the traits a measure was designed to measure, its format, and the possible range of score values.

☐ 9.14 Summarize information on reliability and validity, when available.

☐ 9.15 Provide references where more information on the measures can be found.

☐ 9.16 Consider providing sample items or questions.

☐ 9.17 Make unpublished measures available.

Chapter 10 Describing Experimental Methods

☐ 10.1 Describe experimental methods under the subheading "Procedure" under the main heading of "Method."

☐ 10.2 If there are two or more groups, explicitly state how the groups were formed.

☐ 10.3 Distinguish between *random selection* and *random assignment.*

☐ 10.4 For experiments with only one participant, describe the length of each condition.

☐ 10.5 Describe the experimental treatment in detail.

☐ 10.6 Describe physical controls over the administration of the experimental treatment.

☐ 10.7 Describe the control condition.

☐ 10.8 Describe steps taken to reduce the "expectancy effect."

☐ 10.9 If there was attrition, describe the dropouts.

☐ 10.10 If participants were debriefed, mention it.

Chapter 11 Writing Analysis and Results Sections

☐ 11.1 "Analysis" is a subheading under the main heading of "Method."

☐ 11.2 The Analysis subsection is used sparingly in reports on quantitative research.

☐ 11.3 The Analysis subsection is usually included in reports on qualitative research.

☐ 11.4 "Results" is a main heading that follows the main heading "Method."

☐ 11.5 Organize the Results section around the research hypotheses, objectives, or questions.

☐ 11.6 It is usually not necessary to show formulas or calculations in either the Analysis or Results sections.

☐ 11.7 The scores of individual participants usually are not shown.

☐ 11.8 Present descriptive statistics before inferential statistics.

☐ 11.9 Organize large numbers of statistics in tables or other visuals.

☐ 11.10 Give each table a number and a caption (i.e., a descriptive title).

☐ 11.11 Refer to statistical tables by number within the text of the Results section.

☐ 11.12 When describing the statistics presented in a table or visual, point out only the highlights.

☐ 11.13 Figures (e.g., flow charts, graphs, etc.) should be used sparingly.

☐ 11.14 Statistical symbols should be underlined or italicized.

☐ 11.15 Use the proper case for each statistical symbol.

☐ 11.16 Consider when to spell out numbers.

☐ 11.17 Qualitative results should be organized and the organization made clear to the reader.

Chapter 12 Writing Discussion Sections

☐ 12.1 "Discussion" is a main heading that follows the main heading "Results."

☐ 12.2 Consider starting the Discussion with a summary.

☐ 12.3 Early in the Discussion section, refer to the research hypotheses, objectives, or questions.

☐ 12.4 Point out whether results of the current study are consistent with the literature described in the literature review.

☐ 12.5 Interpret the results and offer explanations for them in the Discussion section.

☐ 12.6 Mention important strengths and limitations in the Discussion section.

☐ 12.7 It is usually inappropriate to introduce new data or new references in the Discussion section.

☐ 12.8 State specific implications in the Discussion section.

☐ 12.9 Be specific when making recommendations for future research.

☐ 12.10 Consider using subheadings within the Discussion section.

Chapter 13 Writing Abstracts

☐ 13.1 Determine the maximum length permissible for an abstract.

☐ 13.2 If space permits, consider beginning an abstract by describing the general problem area.

☐ 13.3 If space is limited, consider beginning by summarizing the research hypotheses, objectives, or questions.

☐ 13.4 Highlights of the methodology should be summarized.

☐ 13.5 Highlights of the results should be included.

☐ 13.6 Point out any unexpected results.

☐ 13.7 If a study is strongly tied to a theory, name the theory in the abstract.

☐ 13.8 Mention any unique aspects of a study.

☐ 13.9 Mention if a line of inquiry is new.

☐ 13.10 If implications and suggestions for future research are emphasized in the report, consider concluding the abstract by mentioning them.

☐ 13.11 An abstract should usually be short; however, there are exceptions.

☐ 13.12 Consider using subheadings in an abstract.

Chapter 14 A Closer Look at Writing Reports of Qualitative or Mixed Methods Research

☐ 14.1 Consider using the term *qualitative* in the title of the report.

☐ 14.2 Consider using the terms *qualitative* or *mixed methods* in the abstract of the report.

☐ 14.3 Consider discussing the choice of qualitative over quantitative methodology.

☐ 14.4 Consider "revealing yourself" to the readers.

☐ 14.5 Avoid calling a sample *purposive* if it is actually a sample of convenience.

☐ 14.6 If a purposive sample was used, state the basis for selection of participants.

☐ 14.7 Describe how participants were recruited.

☐ 14.8 Provide demographic information.

☐ 14.9 Provide specific information on data collection methods.

☐ 14.10 Describe steps taken to ensure the trustworthiness of the data.

☐ 14.11 If two or more researchers participated in analyzing the data, describe how they arrived at a consensus.

☐ 14.12 In the Results section of a qualitative report, provide quantitative results on quantitative matters.

☐ 14.13 Consider using the major themes as subheadings in the Results section.

☐ 14.14 If quotations are reported, consider stating the basis for their selection.

☐ 14.15 Consider discussing alternative interpretations of the data and why they were rejected.

Chapter 15 Preparing Reference Lists

☐ 15.1 "References" is a main heading that follows the main heading "Discussion."

☐ 15.2 Select a style manual and carefully follow its directions for preparing a reference list.

☐ 15.3 A journal title is treated like a book title—italicize it.

☐ 15.4 Double-check punctuation in accordance with the style manual.

☐ 15.5 Double-check capitalization in accordance with the style manual.

☐ 15.6 A reference list should only contain entries for works that have been cited in the research report.

☐ 15.7 Cross-check reference citations in the body of the report with those in the reference list.

Appendix B

Thinking Straight and Writing That Way*

Appendix B presents the first-hand perspective of Ann Robinson, an academic and journal editor who has reviewed and critiqued many research manuscripts.

Everyone who submits manuscripts to top-flight journals gets rejected by the reviewers more than once in his or her publishing career. Often the rejections seem, at best, inexplicable and, at worst, biased. Rejections sting.

In a cooler moment, the disappointed author looks over the rejected paper and tries to read the reviewers' comments more calmly. What do journal reviewers look for in a manuscript? What makes a submission publishable? How can you increase the likelihood that your work will be accepted? These are good questions for any would-be author—seasoned or new—to ask.

In general, sessions on publishing "how-to's" rarely get beyond the obligatory lecture on the importance of the idea. We are told that if the idea is good, we should carry out the research study and proceed to submit the work for publication. If the how-to-get-published session gets past the point of explaining that a good study is one that asks an important question, then we are told that a publishable study is one that is reasonably free of design flaws. It seems to me that these two points ought to be considered givens. Although it is not always easy to think of a good idea, translate it into a researchable question, and design a competent study, most of us already understand the importance of these things. What we want to know now is how to increase our chances of getting competent work published in the *Gifted Child Quarterly*.

Over the last eight years, I have developed the following questions to use when reviewing research manuscripts. They are offered as one reviewer's "test" of the publishability of a manuscript and may be helpful as guides for the prospective *Quarterly* author.

* Originally published in *Gifted Child Quarterly*, *32*(4), 367–369 as "Thinking straight and writing that way: Publishing in *Gifted Child Quarterly*." Copyright 1988 by the National Association for Gifted Children. Reprinted with permission.

Reviewer Question #1: What's the point?

Early on in the first "quick read," I ask why I should be interested in this manuscript. Will this study fill a gap in the existing literature? Will this study reconcile apparently contradictory research results from studies already published? Is this study anchored to a real problem affecting the education and upbringing of gifted children and youth? Is this study "newsworthy"? Does the author convince me in the first few paragraphs that this manuscript is going to present important information new to the field or be investigated from a fresh perspective?

The manuscripts that most effectively make their "point" often have brief introductions that state the essence of the issue in the first or last sentence of the first or second paragraph. As a reviewer, I look for that "essence of issue" sentence. It is a benchmark for clear thinking and writing.

Reviewer Question #2: Can I find the general research question?

Reviewer Question #2 is related to the first, but I am now looking for something a bit more technical. The general research question should be stated clearly, and it should serve as the lodestone for the specific questions generated for the study. Congruence is important here. If I were to take each of these specific questions and check them against the general question, I would easily see the connection. For example, in a study of the family systems of underachieving males, the general question is, "What are the interactional relationships within families of gifted students?" (Green, Fine, & Tollefson, 1988). Two specific questions derived from the general one are:

(1) Is there a difference in the proportion of families of achieving and underachieving gifted that are classified as functional and dysfunctional?
(2) Do family members having achieving or underachieving gifted students differ in their satisfaction with their families?

(p. 268)

The manuscripts which most effectively answered Reviewer Question #2 place the general question at the end of the review of the literature. It will be stated as a question and prefaced with a lead-in like "the general purpose of this study" or "an important research question is." Then the specific questions for the study are enumerated and set apart in a list. The combination of text and visual cues makes it difficult for the reviewer to overlook the focus of the manuscript.

Reviewer Question #3: Can I get a "picture" of the participants of this study?

The appropriate level of description for the participants is difficult to judge. However, it is better to over- rather than underdescribe them. This is true whether the study is experimental or a naturalistic inquiry. Insufficient information about the participants in the study leaves the reviewer wondering if the conclusions are suspect. Would the results be the same if other participants had participated? Go beyond the breakdowns by age or grade, sex, and ethnicity. If the subjects are students in a gifted program, describe the identification procedure. If the subjects are school personnel, describe their professional positions, years in service, or other variables that might affect the results. As a reviewer, I always try to determine the extent to which a subject sample is volunteer and how seriously volunteerism might bias the results. If a study is conducted in one school building, district, or one teacher or parent advocate group, I look for descriptions of this context. How large is the school or organization? Is it rural, urban, or suburban? Who is responding to surveys? Fathers or mothers? Are families intact, single-parent, or extended? What is the socioeconomic level?

For example, in a study of learning styles, Rica (1984) included the following information to give a thorough picture of the subjects:

> The study population included 425 students in grades four, five, and six from one city school and one suburban school district in Western New York. Descriptive contrast groups represented subjects who were identified as gifted and a contrast group taken from the remaining general school students available. Gifted students were identified by a multidimensional screening process with data sources indicated in Table 1.
>
> *(p. 121)*

This information is followed by a further explanation of the identification process and three brief tables that provide a tidy summary of student demographics and cognitive and academic characteristics. The combination of text and tables gives the reviewer a clear picture of the subjects in the study.

The reviewer may ultimately ask the author to trim the text on subjects, but overzealous descriptions serve two purposes. First, they demonstrate to the reviewer that the author is a careful worker. Second, they rein in generalizations, which appear in the Conclusions and Implications sections of the manuscript. An author may well be entitled to make statements about the population from which the sample of participants is drawn, but if the demographics of the group change, the conclusions may not be safely generalized.

The manuscripts that most effectively create a picture of their sample include the basics like age, grade, sex, and ethnicity succinctly, sometimes in tabled form. Case study researchers are less likely to use tables because of smaller samples, but they do identify the reasons why they believe a participant is representative of a large group. In studies of gifted children, the most effective manuscripts clearly state the selection procedure and identify specific instruments or checklists, if appropriate, under the Subjects section of the paper.

Reviewer Question #4: Is this author killing flies with an elephant gun?

As a reviewer, I examine the manuscript for a comfortable fit among the research questions, the kinds of data that have been collected, and the tools of analysis. In the case of manuscripts that present quantitative data and statistical analyses, I apply Occam's razor. The simplest statistics are usually the best. A good research question can be insightfully investigated with relatively simple analyses provided the assumptions are not too badly violated. The purpose of statistics is to summarize and clarify, not to fog.

Of course, authors who seek to control confounded variables through the use of more sophisticated statistical treatments like the currently popular LISREL increase the likelihood that multiple causation is disentangled. We certainly gain from technological innovation; however, the key is to determine if the impetus for the study is a substantive research question or a fascination with the newest techniques.

The manuscripts that answer Reviewer Question #4 most effectively are those in which hypotheses do not sink under the weight of the analyses. As I read the Design and Analysis sections, am I able to keep my eye on the important variables? A good indicator is a sentence in the Design section that gives me the rationale for using quite sophisticated or new statistical and qualitative techniques. For example, a study of ethnic differences in a mathematics program for gifted students included the following explanation for the selection of a specialized kind of regression analysis (Robinson, Bradley, & Stanley, in review):

> Regression discontinuity is a quasi-experimental design that allows the experimenter to test for treatment effects without a randomized control group and the attendant withholding of services. This a priori design statistically controls for prior differences by using the identification variable along with program participation (status) as independent variables in a multiple regression model.
>
> *(p. 7)*

Another indication that the study is being driven by its questions rather than its statistics is the author's effort to make connecting statements between a technique and its interpretation. To return to the previous regression example:

> If the associated t test of the regression coefficient is significant, it is indicative of a program that impacts on its participants.
>
> *(p. 7)*

Reviewer Question #5: Would George Orwell approve?

Dogging the reviewer through both the "quick read" and the "close read" of the manuscript is the ease with which the author has answered the first four questions.

If we look back at those questions, we see the common thread of clarity running through them. What is the point? Where is the question? Who is this study about? Does the analysis illuminate rather than obfuscate?

Reviewer Question #5 is the final test. Would George Orwell approve? In 1946, Orwell published "Politics and the English Language," one of the clearest statements on writing effectively ever to appear in print. The thesis of his essay was that

> modern English, especially written English, is full of bad habits, which spread by imitation and which can be avoided if one is willing to take the necessary trouble ... prose consists less and less of words chosen for the sake of their meaning, and more and more of phrases tacked together like sections of a pre-fabricated hen-house.
>
> *(p. 159)*

Orwell was clearly unhappy with vague writing and professional jargon. He felt that poor writing was an indication of sloppy thinking, and he excused neither the social scientist nor the novelist from his strict dicta of good, vigorous writing. He had a particular dislike of using ready-made phrases like "lay the foundation," and he was equally appalled at the indiscriminate use of scientific terms to give the impression of objectivity to biased statements.

As a reviewer, I apply Orwell's tough rules to the test of every manuscript I receive. It means that the manuscript author has answered Reviewer Questions 1 through 4 successfully. According to Orwell,
the following rules will cover most cases:

1. Never use a metaphor, simile, or other figure of speech which you are used to seeing in print.
2. Never use a long word where a short one will do.
3. If it is possible to cut a word out, always cut it out.
4. Never use the passive where you can use the active.
5. Never use a foreign phrase, a scientific word, or a jargon word if you can think of an everyday English equivalent.
6. Break any of these rules sooner than say anything outright 'barbarous'.

(p. 170)

Orwell had the good sense to include the sixth rule as a disclaimer. All writers make errors and violate rules, sometimes out of carelessness, sometimes for effect. It is also true that writing for highly specialized journals does require the judicious use of technical language, just as sheep shearers need specialized terms to describe differing grades of wool. However, moderation in the use and the arbitrary, spontaneous creation of specialized vocabulary is certainly warranted in our field. It is refreshing to read an author who states that the subjects in the study are "thinking critically" rather than "realizing greater cognitive gains."

Orwell makes many fine points about the importance of sincerity in thinking and writing. For the prospective social science writer, none are more important than the careful selection and lively use of technical terms. I know of no more rigorous test to apply to a manuscript than to ask if George Orwell would approve. Passing this "test" means the author is thinking straight and writing that way.

References

Green, K., Fine, M. J., & Tollefson, N. (1988). Family systems characteristics and under-achieving gifted adolescent males. *Gifted Child Quarterly, 32*, 267–276.

Orwell, G. (1953). Politics and the English language. In G. Orwell (Ed.), *A Collection of Essays* (pp. 156–171). San Diego: Harcourt, Brace, Jovanovich.

Rica, J. (1984). Learning styles and preferred instructional strategies. *Gifted Child Quarterly, 28*, 121–126.

Robinson, A., Bradley, R., & Stanley, T. D. (in review). Opportunity to achieve: The identification and performance of Black students in a program for the mathematically talented.

The Null Hypothesis and Significance Testing

Formal significance testing begins with the *null hypothesis*. This is a statistical hypothesis that asserts that any differences researchers observe when studying random samples are the result of random (chance) errors created by the random sampling. For instance, suppose a researcher asked a random sample of men from some population and a random sample of women from the same population whether they supported legalizing physician-assisted suicide for the terminally ill and found that 51% of the women supported it while only 49% of the men supported it. At first, the researcher might be tempted to report that women are more supportive of this proposition than men are. However, the null hypothesis warns us that the 2-percentage-point difference between women and men may have resulted solely from sampling errors. In other words, there may be no difference between men and women in the population—the researcher may have found a difference because he or she administered the questionnaire to only these two particular samples.

Of course, it is also possible that the men and women in the population are truly different in their opinion on physician-assisted suicide, and the population difference is responsible for the difference between the percentages for the two samples. In other words, the samples may accurately reflect the gender difference in the population. This possibility is called an *alternative hypothesis* (i.e., an alternative to the null hypothesis).

Which hypothesis is correct? It turns out that the only way to answer this question is to test the null hypothesis. If the test indicates that a researcher may reject the null hypothesis, then they will be left with only the alternative hypothesis as an explanation. When a researcher rejects the null hypothesis, they say that they have identified a *reliable* difference—one that can be relied on because it probably is not just an artifact of random errors.

Through a set of computational procedures that are beyond the scope of this book, a significance test results in a *probability that the null hypothesis is true*. The symbol for this probability is p. By conventional standards, when the probability that the null hypothesis is true is as low as or lower than 5 in 100, researchers reject the null hypothesis. (Note that a low probability means that it is unlikely that the null hypothesis is true. If something is *unlikely* to be true, researchers reject it as a possibility.)

The formal term that researchers use when discussing the rejection of the null hypothesis is *statistical significance*. For example, the following two statements might appear in the Results section of a research report:

> The difference between the means for the liberals and conservatives is statistically significant ($p < .05$).

> The difference between the means for the men and women is not statistically significant ($p > .05$).

The first statement says that the probability that the null hypothesis is true is less than (<) 5 in 100; thus, the null hypothesis is rejected, and the difference is declared to be *statistically significant*. The second statement says that the probability that the null hypothesis is true is greater than (>) 5 in 100; thus, the null hypothesis is *not* rejected, and the difference is *not statistically significant*.

In other words, significance tests help researchers make decisions based on the odds that something is true. All individuals do this in their everyday lives. For example, when preparing to cross a busy street, you look at oncoming cars to judge their speed and distance to see if it is safe to cross. If you decide that there is a *low probability* that you will be able to cross the street safely, you *reject* the hypothesis that it is safe to cross the street.

Index

Pages followed by "n" refer to notes.

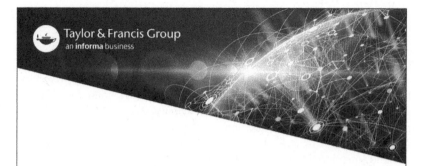